Lifestorm

By

Denise P. Kalm

ISBN: 0-7596-7580-5

This book is printed on acid free paper.

1stBooks - rev. 11/29/01

To my mother, Louise Kalm Hitchcock, who wrested courage from the ashes to build a new life.

God gave Noah the rainbow sign

No more water, the fire next time.

— Anonymous

PROLOGUE

"Fire is the test of gold; adversity of strong men."

— Seneca

Neil Grossman barked into his car phone once more, then fumbled to hook up his portable fax machine. "Sending," he muttered, mostly to himself since the phone was tied up digitizing the message. Not for the first time, he asked himself how he had gotten trapped in sales, conning people. Twenty-five years ago, as a college student, he had wanted to make a difference in people's lives, not just sell them hardware.

Heading west from the bedroom community of Orinda to San Francisco, he slowed the speed of his black Lexus, trying to send the last line before entering the Caldecott Tunnel. "Can't do a bit of work in here," he muttered. "What were they thinking of when they built this thing?" He could get a lot done on Sundays…usually. Too many nights and weekends spent this way had etched lines through the old acne scars on his cheeks and forehead. He blamed the sales quotas for his thinning hair; he had been darkening the gray for years with a comb-in color solution.

Neil's car sped downhill out of the tunnel into a wall of black smoke. He hit the brakes hard and the car slewed sideways, crossing several lanes before he regained control. Headlights glared, spilling their light into the ashes. Cars jolted over the dirt from the access roads, crossing in front of him, trying to escape the fire that raged down the hillside. Tires squealed, horns honked frantically, sounds emerging out of nowhere. Narrowly avoiding the cross traffic, Neil edged to the shoulder and parked. He forced himself to take long, deep breaths, willing his hands to stop shaking.

His line of sight was blocked by the large "Parkwoods Apartments" sign and the heavy, gray cement blocks fronting on the freeway. Oh, God! Mary! His best friend and confidante since college lived in one of those units. The only one who really knew who he was, who he wanted to be. Neil tried to imagine how his friend would escape. In a wheelchair, she couldn't manage alone. Who would help her? He had to get inside.

It had to be bad at Parkwoods; most of the cars he'd narrowly missed hitting had come from Caldecott Lane, next to the guard station. Mary's building was set midway into the cleft of the hill - she could be trapped. As he ran into the apartment complex, the buildings to the back were obscured by the smoke - no chance for any of them, he thought.

His throat ached at the harsh tang of the oxygen-starved smoke, and he was barely able to see. He tried to remember what he had learned years before, as a medic in Viet Nam. He had saved men from worse situations than this. Fighting his way through a tide of people, Neil paused to dip his handkerchief in a pond next to the first building and pressed it to his lips. It helped, a little. Squinting, he tried to assess the situation.

The fire swept down from the hills, working its way to the buildings in the center of the complex. He could barely see Mary's building. Whispering a silent prayer for her safety, he counted fire trucks - too few. Parkwoods had no chance.

Heading closer, Neil noticed a young woman and child, crouched on a third floor balcony in one of the buildings close to the exit. It could be Mary's apartment... It looked like her... But who was the child?

He raced to the stairs, bolting them two at a time, only to find himself barred by a locked, metal door. He sprinted to the lobby, where he knew he could break in through the glass. No choice - he had to trust the elevator. The fire had just reached this building, and the burning synthetic materials fumed, making his lungs ache. His eyes burned. He could barely make out the floor numbers.

Fighting his way through the hallway, Neil cried out, pounding on each door as he passed. Which one was it? He couldn't read the numbers through the smoke. Finally, he reached an open door and pushed through. He tripped on a chair as he felt his way to the balcony. Mary clutched the child, crying, pointing to her wheelchair. It was caught on something. He couldn't free it. Oh, God, it was her! He called out her name, but she didn't recognize him. No time.

Choking on the smoky air, he hoisted her to his back, hoping she had the strength to cling to him. Her legs dangled, heavy. He lifted the sturdy three-year-old with difficulty and staggering under the weight, tried to run. The child screamed and squirmed; Neil held him harder, wanting to stop the wails. Could he do this? An explosion rocked the building, throwing them to the floor. Before he could get up, he felt the building shudder. Neil grabbed the two again, then half-slid down the stairs, his feet barely making contact with the cement risers.

He ran in front of a car, forcing it to stop. Gasping for air, he helped the two into it, then watched as the car shot through the gate. Neil returned to the building, still hearing cries from inside. "It's unsafe... I can't go in there again... It's coming down on my head," he argued with himself. But he had to. People were still trapped in there. He couldn't leave them.

Neil took the elevator again, cursing the security measures that turned buildings like this into deathtraps. He listened for the screams - fainter now. "Cement doesn't burn," he told himself. "I have nothing to worry about." Flames began to catch at his loose shirt.

Finally, he found the source of the noise - a Siamese cat, wailing its distress in a baby-like yowl. He caught up the animal, running. The floor exploded upward, catching his legs in the cracks. He felt the flesh on his back begin to sear, and tried to loosen the cat's claws. "Go! Run!" he cried, thrusting the cat through the narrow crack to the ground floor.

Neil struggled, sure he could break through the floor and get free, but there was no air left to breathe, and no way to put out the flames that wreathed his skull. He took a long last gasp of the poisoned air, and died.

CHAPTER 1

"Cruel firestorm turns an Eastbay paradise into a raging hell on earth."
— Oakland Tribune
10/21/91

Amanda Dunn eased the lounging pajama jacket over her reddening, tender shoulders, deciding it was time to come in from the balcony, probably past time. Sweat beaded on her forehead, and the ice-blue silk molded itself to her body in the moist, Hawaiian heat. She liked the rich gold of a tropical tan contrasting with her blonde hair, but she was usually too impatient to take it slowly.

Amanda checked her Piaget watch, then picked up the Day-Timer Jeff insisted on using, even on vacation. It was only 1:00; plenty of time for a shower and a few minutes of TV before Jeff would be back from his golf game. She sighed. Golf had become the salvation for their marriage. As trip planner and travel agent for the couple, she had found that the best vacations were those where she scheduled time for separate activities. Destinations with challenging golf courses were at the top of her list. Jeff had been happy to buy the ocean-view condo in Kihei, a place they both enjoyed. He spent his mornings miles away in Kaanapali, allowing her plenty of time to read, walk the empty beaches or just sit and think, activities Jeff wouldn't share.

She never understood his need to have all his activities planned in advance, even on weekends. Amanda preferred to leave her watch behind, letting life just happen to her. Keeping track of hours at the law office - billable hours - was enough. Of course, Jeff never let her forget the time; a well-planned schedule soothed him.

Amanda took a moment to admire the cozy retreat she had designed for the two of them. The colors reflected sea and sand; she let her imagination run wild. She reserved part of each trip for shopping, selecting the best the islands had to offer - wicker and teak furniture, art treasures from the gallery at Kilauea, fresh island flowers to add a note of color. The vases were Oriental, shipped from Gump's in San Francisco.

Amanda's mother had been a collector too, but their house was a rummage-sale, hodge podge of whatever caught her eye and could be had cheaply. Warm and comfortable, but never stylish. Amanda liked to believe that Architectural Digest could drop in on either of her homes at any moment and find a creation worth photographing.

Flipping channels on the big screen TV, she located a news show, then settled her sensitive back carefully against a pile of pillows on the queen bed. She watched with one eye, focusing the other on her nails. The emery board took care of an imperceptible unevenness; she then began to pick at some errant polish on her cuticles. The talking heads chattered about the weather, a subject of little interest to her or most California natives.

"We interrupt this program to bring you a special bulletin."

Amanda groaned and went to the kitchen to get a can of diet soda. She didn't think she'd care, even if it was a report that Haleakala was about to spew hot lava down on Kihei. The tropical humidity had baked her mind and muscles into a lethargic state. She half-listened to the news report, while she dealt with the problem of lifting the pop-top with a knife. Jeff liked her long, glimmering, useless nails.

"Hello. I'm Ngaio Minh, reporting from the Bay Area community of Oakland, California. A major fire is sweeping through the thickly forested hill area, fueled by unseasonably high winds and the multi-year drought. This fire appears to be a recurrence of Saturday's small brush fire, thought to be under control when the Oakland Fire Department left it. It is unclear at this time why the fire re-ignited, or what caused the original blaze."

Horrified, Amanda dropped the can of soda and rushed into the bedroom. The picture shifted from the newswoman to a panorama of smoky air, ripped through by orange-red flames.

The newscaster's bland voice continued to describe the situation, but Amanda only heard scattered words..." out of control..." "losses in the millions..." "victims..." "fatalities..."

She watched, unblinking, fascinated by the collage of dancing red flames and inky smoke. In the premature night sky, only vague silhouettes gave any indication of houses in the conflagration. Footage shifted to people, madly careening down the hills in cars, tires melting, horns blaring. Trees exploded into flame as the fire swept down one hill, then leapt across the street into another valley. Amanda recognized a clubhouse, a swimming pool, a large chimney.

3

A scream caught in her throat, held back only by her clenched teeth and the fist jammed against her mouth. The camera had caught the image of her own Hiller Highlands home bursting into flame. She stared, hypnotized. Amanda felt suddenly detached, as if the picture on the television was only a trick of computer graphics, not relating to reality at all.

A eucalyptus fragmented in a sudden whoosh; she emitted a strangled laugh. The picture blurred into abstract images and the words of the newswoman were only jarring noise. Disembodied voices screamed, fire trucks shrieked. Amanda watched as the wall of fire swept down the hill, selecting this house, leaving another, like a deranged demolition squad.

"It's not our house. It can't be," she told herself. "I didn't really see it... It was dark... Probably a hundred houses look just like it... Someone else's, not mine." Amanda looked back at the screen, ordering herself not to worry until she saw it again.

As the scene shifted to the area above Highway 13, she began to watch for friends' neighborhoods and to worry about her mother. Ruth Creighton lived alone in a wood-framed cottage in Montclair. But the fire couldn't have gotten that far, could it?

Amanda didn't know she was crying until she licked the salt of it from her lips. What do I do now? I mean, what do we do now?

*   *   *

Jeffrey Dunn was in a good mood, a very good mood. The Kaanapali course that had him tossing his clubs at trees last year had been a snap today. At this rate, he might drop his handicap into the single digits. His pickup partner had been very impressed; Jeff modestly credited his new graphites.

He entered their condo whistling, ready to sustain Amanda on a flurry of shopping, or even to spend the rest of the day locked up in some museum; she always liked that. He caught himself in the mirror and shucked off the sweat-stained Izod shirt. Sucking in his stomach, he admired his torso. Not bad for an old guy, he told himself.

Jeff found his wife frozen in shock in front of the television, her makeup streaked under her eyes. She didn't seem to know that he was in the room.

He shook her shoulder roughly, unsettled at her emotional state. It had only been a couple of hours, he thought. What is her problem? He never knew what to say to bring her out of a funk, and Amanda generally wouldn't make much of an effort herself. What had he done this time?

Shock and pain-filled eyes stared up at him, when she finally acknowledged his presence.

"What's wrong?" Jeff asked abruptly, regretting the words even as they left his lips. He knew it would set her off.

"Don't you care what happens to us?" Amanda moaned.

Care? Wasn't that why we went on this vacation - the worst time of year for his business - because he knew she needed a break?

"Of course I do." God, does every talk have to be a relationship talk? "What's the problem, honey?"

"Our house is gone," she said. "I saw it. At least, I think I did." Amanda jumped up to mash the channel buttons until she located another news broadcast on the fire; Jeff shook his head, staring at her. She was transfixed by the flames, as fascinated by the sight as a rubbernecking driver. He sat down next to her, slipping his arm around her gently. She pulled away.

It took him a while to understand what he was seeing. Jeff didn't recognize his own neighborhood in the sooty flames, what was left of it. The artificial dusk of ash made it even harder to determine the extent of the fire. A list of the devastated streets scrolled down the screen, and even though he already knew, Jeff waited until he saw the black and white proof of his loss.

Amanda began to shake, gut-wrenching tears surging up again. Jeff held her until rage overcame his inertia and drove him to the phone.

"They'll pay for this," he stormed. "Damn it, with what we pay in taxes, this should never have happened."

Amanda ignored his outburst, which enraged him even more.

"We'd better fly out tonight," Jeff said, as he dialed United Airlines. "Sure as hell, we can't trust the city government to handle this. And FEMA..." He groaned, remembering the way they handled the '89 earthquake. Santa Cruz still looked like a war zone.

Moving like a robot, Amanda rose and began throwing clothes into their suitcases. She ignored his sputterings as he fought with the agent over their non-refundable tickets.

"I don't care what it costs. Just get us out of here." Jeff slammed the phone down.

He paced the length of their living room, picking up objects, then setting them down aimlessly. The sound of a candlestick thrown against the wall startled Amanda. She dropped the shirt she had scrunched up, while really meaning to fold it carefully.

6

"Jeff?" She looked scared.

Jeff gripped the cold metal balcony and stared out over the water. His voice came out in icy tones, sharp enough to etch glass. "Everything we've worked for - gone. Someone has to pay. They can't do this to me."

CHAPTER 2

"In Oakland and San Francisco, a plume of choking black smoke turned the sun orange and turned daylight into an eerie murky twilight."

— Craig Staats/Carolyn Newbergh
Oakland Tribune

The Dunn's flight was late. They grabbed the last two seats in the crowded gate area and watched the other passengers badger the gate agents with the urgency of their return. Brown-edged leis hung around the necks of a few, framing faces that were already back home with their problems and worries.

Amanda pointed to one old woman, who clutched a bag nearly half her size. The agent was trying to pry her fingers loose; the bag was too big to carry on.

"Jeff, look. You'd think she had all her possessions in that one bag and the airline was trying to steal it from her."

Jeff chuckled, then the sound caught in his throat. "We do, honey. We just checked everything we own. Gives a whole new meaning to losing your luggage." Jeff remembered how easily he had tossed their large pieces on the scale to be checked.

"Where do we go when we land? We can't very well go home, whatever home is," Amanda asked, still trying to hold back hysterical laughter.

"Well, we could camp out, if you hadn't left the tents in the garage."

Initially irritated by Amanda's tendency to see the funny side of it, Jeff found odd thoughts of his own rising to his tongue. "Are you sorry you spent so much time cleaning before we left?" His eyes twinkled as he twitted her on one of her obsessions.

"Think what the firemen would have said if I hadn't vacuumed," she fired back.

Though the terminal area was crowded, people began to give a wide berth to the couple; their laughter was almost maniacal. Amanda noticed and the sight of people edging away from them just made her laugh more. "If we keep this up, we can have a whole section of the plane to ourselves," she said.

"Do we make you uncomfortable?" Jeff tossed out the words to the crowd, then dug his elbow into Amanda's side, the part of her most easily tickled. Initially uncomfortable with the attention, Jeff found he enjoyed getting in people's faces while maintaining the anonymity of a traveler. They don't know what to do with us, he thought. We aren't playing our assigned roles.

Passengers edged toward the ramp, still keeping their distance. The normal herding tendency was disrupted as Jeff led Amanda to the doorway. He felt like Moses, watching the rows part to let them pass.

"I think they want to see where we're sitting," Amanda said, still giggling.

Jeff shook his head. Sheep. The whole lot of them. How many of them cared what they were going through, even questioned their assumption that they were flying with crazies?

Business class was not full. They found a few extra seats, so Amanda could stretch out, with her head on Jeff's lap. Exhausted, they both slept, dreamlessly ignoring the movie, the snack and the free drinks they normally enjoyed.

*   *   *

Luggage spewed out of the hole in the center of the carousel, spreading garment bags, boxes and suitcases onto the track like lava. The Dunns lined up along the belt, just another pair of rumpled tourists, stale from sleeping in the dry air of their flight. It was 8:30 AM, but it felt like 5. Amanda gripped her small carry-on tightly, unwilling to set it down next to her. Signs posted prominently in the San Francisco Airport warned of baggage thieves, and with no one to check claim tags, they usually got away with it.

Watching their matched pieces moving slowly toward them, Amanda couldn't help measuring up their net worth in terms of the luggage - it represented everything they owned. Bathing suits, tee-shirts, souvenirs… But most of it was new. They had splurged on resort wear for this vacation; there was nothing old or familiar about any of it. Oh, yes. Jeff's shirt. The faded Hawaiian print shirt with the tacky palm trees and hula girls dated back to their first visit to Oahu, when they could only dream of buying a condo for vacations. On that trip, they squeezed into coach seats and stayed in a lodge several blocks from the beach - economies Jeff felt were necessary to enable him to build up his investment portfolio. His divorce had been costly. The shirt was the only souvenir he allowed himself to buy. Amanda had tried unsuccessfully to throw the shirt out, or give it away. Jeff always managed to salvage it. Now, she envied him having a shirt softened and age-imbued with all those memories.

Jeff reached past her, trying to grab their bags, which appeared to speed up as they moved past him.

"Damn. Why does all our luggage have to come off at the same time?" He vented his frustration by flinging two heavy bags at Amanda's feet. She ignored them, leaving him to push past others to snatch at the last two escaping suitcases.

"Do something," Jeff ordered. "Find a cart... something."

Amanda looked at him, as if she had just become aware of his presence. She wrestled a cart near him, then set the only light bag, her tote, on it.

"No. Not that way," Jeff said, with a huff of impatience. "Big, heavy stuff on the bottom, small stuff on top." He pushed her tote off with his foot, then organized the stacking to his satisfaction.

"Do you think you could handle pushing the cart out to the street? I'll get the car." The zany mood of the night before was gone. He left at a trot, trying to catch the parking lot shuttle as it pulled away from the curb.

Amanda nodded to him, then tried to give the cart a shove. The wheel caught on a loose strap of the luggage. She tore a fingernail off below the quick trying to free it. Drops of blood welled up.

"Oh, shit." Amanda barely held in a choking sob. What's wrong with me, she asked herself. It's just a nail, damn it. It hurt, but that wasn't what brought on the tears. She dug through her purse, finally finding a crumpled, but unused Band-Aid. She wrapped it carefully around the ragged edge of the nail. Amanda placed the sculptured nail tip into her wallet for safekeeping, then began to laugh.

"I wonder if the manicure salon is still there," she mused. Still, the small tip seemed precious to her - a small thing that represented life before the fire.

The luggage - I've got to get it out to the street. She waved to a sky cap who smiled and swung the cart effortlessly to the curb. Jeff was waiting; the trunk was already open.

"Where have you been? Having coffee?" Jeff asked, flinging the luggage into the car.

"I broke a nail," she said, showing him her bandaged finger.

Jeff rolled his eyes. He tossed a few dollars in the general direction of the sky cap, then slid quickly into the driver's seat. Amanda stopped briefly to pick up the scattered bills and handed them to the porter.

"Thank you," she said, flushing with embarrassment for Jeff.

"Okay. Where do we go now?" Jeff muttered. "We can't go home."

"Maybe we should go look at our house," Amanda suggested.

"At what? A pile of ashes? What good does that do? Besides, the fire is still burning. They won't let us near it."

"Well, maybe we could call the Red Cross. They might have some ideas." Amanda offered her thought, but didn't expect a positive response. Calling the Red Cross was like asking for directions at a gas station. Jeff wouldn't do it.

"Later. I want a home base. We need to have some place to sleep in, at least for the next few days."

"A motel?"

"If there are any. Remember, we don't know how bad it was."

But they did know, Amanda thought. They had watched nothing else since they knew, and Jeff had even bought a portable TV so he could keep CNN on while they waited for the plane.

"I need to find out about Mom. I keep calling, but no one answers," Amanda spoke quietly. "Her house was in the fire zone. We still don't know if it burned." Her voice cracked, sounding strained.

Jeff took her hand. "It's worse for you, isn't it? The not-knowing. You know, she's probably okay. Montclair got a lot of warning."

"But how do we know for sure?"

"She's got loads of friends. I bet she's staying with them now, worrying about you."

Amanda nodded. She had to be okay. Her neighbors would have made sure she got out safely. She clutched the thought in her mind. Believe it, and it will be true.

"Let's find a motel first. Then we can call around," Jeff suggested. "Not much point in calling anyone until we have a phone number. It's going to be okay." He patted her knee, then focused again on driving.

Just then, their car emerged from the lower deck of the Bay Bridge and they saw the blackened hills dotted with charred tree skeletons, chimneys and house frames. Amanda choked. "It's gone. There's nothing there."

"Wait. Look." Jeff stopped the car. Through the smoke, the glistening white of the Claremont Hotel shone like a beacon. "The old hotel made it, so far."

Amanda smiled. "I'm glad. I don't know how they managed with all that wood." More than anything else, the

Claremont Hotel had always signaled "home" to them and to their neighbors. "If it survived, then maybe…"

Jeff shook his head. "No, Amanda."

They noticed the perimeter of the fire, and the odd intact house in the midst of the wreckage. They drove the last few miles in silence, unable to tear their eyes away from the alien landscape.

*   *   *

Ruth Creighton woke slowly in an unfamiliar bed. She was still groggy, but uncomfortably aware of the dampness on her cheek and pillow. I must have slept with my mouth open again, she thought. But why? I only do that when I take my medicine. Her silver hair felt dry and stiff. So did her body, the remembered ache of workouts twenty years ago. The dull throbbing didn't explain why she couldn't move her arms or legs. In willing a leaden arm to move, she felt it stick to the sheet. Why? What had happened to her? Cool air blew gently across her face, and she struggled to see where she was through the thick plastic of the oxygen tent.

Ruth became aware of another person in the room - a young nurse, looked like a new graduate. The nurse gripped her hand gently as she saw her patient's eyes open and begin to register her surroundings.

"Do you know where you are, Mrs. Creighton?"

"I know I'm not home," she said. "Home… Oh, no!" Ruth began remembering a nightmare of smoke and flame, the worst images she had ever dreamed up. "My cat… Where's my cat?" She choked, feeling the hot air as if it were still filling her lungs, burning her. Her eyes teared and ached.

"You're in a hospital, Mrs. Creighton," Nurse Brightman said. "The bandages on your arms and legs are protecting the burned areas on your body. You were lucky to make it out in time."

Ruth tried to sit up, but the pain radiated down her body, making it impossible to lift her head high enough to look at herself. "It really happened? The fire... I didn't dream the fire?" she said, trying to cling to a shred of hope. The memories were beginning to slip in under the drug-induced curtain in her mind. She pushed them back. I'm not ready. I'm 60 years old and I want this woman to tell me that I just had a bad dream.

"Yes, the fire was real," Sandra Brightman began, speaking slowly, as if she were trying to find the words that would blunt the point of the message. "You're okay. That's the important thing. You are going to be just fine. Do you remember being rescued? Two handsome firemen brought you in, just before I went off-shift."

The medication began to wear off, leaving Ruth in even greater pain. It was as if her body was once again covered in flames, eating the skin off as she lay there. "Give me something for the pain," she pleaded. "It's so awful."

The nurse prepared the syringe she had brought with her, just in case her patient was awake. "You have to tell me when you are hurting. We can minimize it for you. Especially when we change your dressings. That can hurt - you just have to tell us."

Ruth nodded, breathing slowly, in through the nose, out through her mouth, letting the medicine do its work. As the pain receded, she tensed. "My daughter. I need to tell my daughter where I am. She's going to worry. I can't remember where she is. Why isn't she here?"

"Tell me her number; I'll call her. Her, and anyone else you like. Just tell me." Sandra reached for a pad of paper in her pocket, noting that it was filled with similar phone number promises. "We would have called immediately, but we didn't find an address book."

As Sandra began to write, she glanced down at her patient. She tucked the pad away. Mrs. Creighton had closed her eyes again, giving in to the medicine and her exhaustion.

Sandra looked down at her patient. One very gutsy lady. The paramedics who brought her in had mentioned that she had to be dragged from her front lawn and the garden hose forcibly pried from her hand, as she tried to save her home. Her clothes had been smoldering, starting to melt into her skin.

Mrs. Creighton would need to be strong, and she would have to want to live. The doctors had expressed their doubts. The tissue damage was deep and the fluid loss serious. Sandra knew that it was up to her to help this woman fight for life, to realize that she was special. She had done it before, with other patients the doctors were too quick to give up on. Sandra held Mrs. Creighton's one unbandaged hand gently, then brushed some of the singed hair away from her face. The worst part was lying to Mrs. Creighton about how serious her condition was, but that was doctor's orders. The nurse hurried off, making a mental note to find Mrs. Creighton's daughter as soon as possible.

CHAPTER 3

"The fire's toll continued to climb. An estimated 2,000 houses and apartments have burned to the ground, 1,800 acres are scorched, and 4,000 to 5,000 people have been left homeless. Another 5,000 people have been evacuated.

"The death toll - 14 confirmed fatalities so far - could go higher when the coroner's teams are able to search through the rubble for additional bodies. Sources say at least 25 people are still missing."

— Harry Harris/Craig Staats
Oakland Tribune

Elaine Freeman stared at the set, keeping her eyes on the picture, even while she reheated some dried-hard lasagna brought home from a restaurant perhaps a week ago. The vivid scenes mesmerized her, as few TV offerings ever had. It was compelling in its dreadfulness. The huddled survivors clutching a blanket, or a rescued pet - all they had left. Elaine found herself touching her possessions, most of little real value, but so substantially hers. Cars squatted in melting-metal traffic jams. Behind it all, the blood-red sun stared down at the alien landscape.

Easier to think of the fire as alien, easier to tell yourself it couldn't happen to you, Elaine thought. But as names and faces scrolled across the screen, she recognized friends from Berkeley and Montclair, other 30-somethings, just like her, losing the first house they'd ever owned. If it happened to them, it could have been her suddenly rendered homeless. Nothing scared her more than that.

Knowing the futility of the effort, Elaine picked up the phone again and began dialing from the list of numbers she had compiled from her address book. She listened to the dial tone echo endlessly. All my friends live in the East Bay, she thought. All of them.

Elaine shivered. It could have been me, she told herself. It almost had been. She had lusted after an old, wood-paneled view home in Berkeley, but couldn't manage the mortgage or the local, liberal politics. For the first time, she could thank the circumstances that put her in the Noe Valley flat, safely moated by the San Francisco Bay. San Francisco was expensive, but a condo in the city suited her independent nature. No roofs to replace, no need of a roommate to help pay the rent. But earthquakes could wipe out my security just as easily as a fire, she thought. And fires follow earthquakes. No one is safe.

Elaine rummaged through her pantry, pulling out a bag of chips she had bought for a party that never happened. I'm eating too much. I always eat when I'm upset. She reached into the bag again and her fingers met only the foil liner. Crumpling the bag, she wiped oily fingers on her tight jeans. She blessed the heredity that kept her frame slim, despite the occasional stress-induced binge.

The phone rang and Elaine froze.

*   *   *

The phone rang on. "Please answer. Please be home," Amanda whispered softly.

"Hello?"

"Elaine. It's me, Amanda." She paused. "You know, don't you?" She couldn't say the words.

"I'm so sorry. I saw it... I thought I saw your house on TV."

"That's how I found out. In Maui, none of it felt real," Amanda said.

"Do you have some place to go?"

"Yes, no... God, I'm just so tired. We're at a motel...someplace. There's smoke everywhere."

"I know. There's even ash blowing around downtown, and I can see a black cloud blocking out the lights on your side. Like an awful fog," Elaine said. "Look, why don't the two of you come here? The air's cleaner and you could get away from it for a while."

Amanda began to laugh. "Get away from what? There's no there, here. Someone said that, didn't they? I would love to see you, but I don't know. Jeff says he's settled for now. I guess he thinks we can do something if we're close."

"Ask him. There's nothing you can do tonight. You need to get out of the smoke."

Amanda covered the mouthpiece of the phone with her hand. "Jeff, Elaine has invited us to stay with her in the City."

"That's big of her."

Amanda frowned. That's right - Jeff didn't like Elaine. He much preferred their other friends, the married ones. Was he afraid of being around a good-looking, single woman? Elaine's ivory skin and dark brown hair might be an exciting change from her own blonde prettiness.

19

"Can we go? I'd like to get away," she said. And pretend that none of this ever happened, she thought to herself.

"Suit yourself," Jeff said. "I'm staying here."

Amanda squeezed back the tears - anger, the only way she could ever show it - glad that Elaine couldn't see her. Shouldn't they stick together right now?

"It's only one night," she said to Jeff. "Couldn't we both go?"

"We've already paid for the room. Someone has to use it." Jeff's tone was even, controlled.

"Would you like me to stay here?"

"I couldn't care less."

Amanda hated him when he withdrew like that. She uncovered the receiver.

"Can you pick me up? Jeff doesn't want to come and we have only the one car." Why did Jeff's Mercedes have to burn up? But he would never have let us leave his baby in the airport parking lot.

"Right away, hon, if you want to go," Elaine said.

"Sure. I guess I'm already packed," Amanda said, grimly eyeing her suitcases. "I could use a nightgown."

Jeff ignored her as she repaired her makeup, going into his sulk-mode, as he did whenever she didn't follow his lead. Amanda realized that she usually let him set the pace; she loved him enough to let him have his way. Most of the things they argued about just didn't matter that much to her. This did. Amanda kissed the top of his head as she prepared to leave. It felt odd to go while they were still fighting. They always talked it out, didn't they?

But this wasn't about them, about the relationship. Maybe he needed some space. But she couldn't remember more than one or two nights they had spent apart since they were married...separated...a separation. Suddenly, Amanda didn't want to leave. Please ask me to stay. Please.

Jeff flopped back on the squishy motel bed and buried his nose in a book. Amanda noticed that it was a book she had bought during the long wait at the Honolulu airport - "Needful Things," the new Stephen King. He hated horror novels, or so he said. Jeff usually had a sensible assortment of trade journals and golf magazines with him; items he was happy to leave in the trash when he was finished. Amanda enjoyed the excuse vacations gave her to read something fun, which at this point amounted to anything that wasn't about the law. She hadn't even been able to dip into the Grisham book she'd bought. Too much like work.

As she left the room, Jeff waved to Amanda from behind the book shield; she felt his gaze on her back. She didn't turn around, couldn't, or she would never leave.

* * *

Leslie Dunn slammed the handset back down on the phone. "All circuits are busy. Try again later." The pleasant recorded voice was grated on her. How long had she been trying to call her father? It seemed like hours.

It was 3 AM in Paris and she had class tomorrow, today actually. Leslie cursed the long distance company and the news agencies who provided such sketchy information about the fire in Oakland. Was Dad okay? What does this endless ringing mean? Is he home? Is there even a house at the end of the line? Who else can I call?

She was surprised to find tears when she rubbed her sleep-starved eyes. Leslie tried to control her breathing, which had become shallow and rapid. Her ash-blonde hair clumped in dark, sweaty strands. Was he gone... No, I can't think of that...not yet. He needs me... I have to get home... Who else does he have?

Damn her. Not for the first time, Leslie cursed her stepmother, Amanda, the sole reason she wasn't home now. Amanda wanted it to be the two of them, alone. The Sorbonne had been a payoff. "Time to try out your wings, Leslie," she had said, but she really meant, "Get out. He's not yours anymore."

But he had been. Ever since Mom - Mother had started drinking, Leslie had been the one to fix meals for her father, sitting up with him and sharing his day. She supported him on the divorce, too. Whatever he wanted. She never dreamed he would want anyone else.

Maybe they weren't home yet. There's hope, she thought, reminding herself of the postcard that had just arrived. If they're still in Maui, he's okay. But if they went home... When? When were they flying back?

Leslie dug through a jumbled stack of papers, looking for his last long letter. Paper flew everywhere, but her eyes couldn't focus, couldn't tell the difference between a phone bill and a letter. Sleep was essential, if she could only close her eyes and not think. There was nothing more she could do now.

The thin veneer of Parisian sophistication she had cultivated was in shreds. She wanted her father, even if it meant trying again with Amanda.

Dragging an afghan off the couch, Leslie curled up in the living room with the phone near at hand. She opened it to the airline listings and put a bookmark at the page. Tomorrow she could try to deal with this, maybe even go home.

CHAPTER 4

"Loss and possession, death and life are one.
There falls no shadow where there shines no sun."

— Hilaire Belloc

"Butchie?" The cry rang out in the quiet of the hospital ward. A passing nurse hurried to Ruth Creighton's bedside and smoothed her hair, blotting her tears gently with a tissue. When her patient was quiet again, Jenny Benson returned to her station.

"How's Mrs. Creighton doing tonight?" the other night nurse asked.

"Pain-wise, as well as can be expected. But she's calling for her cat, Butchie. I don't know what to tell her, Stephanie." Jenny shook her head, making her black curls dance. Losing a pet would be the hardest thing for her. Hazel, her Scottish Fold, was her dearest friend.

"A lot of cats got out. They seemed to have the best survival instinct of any animal caught in the fire. The Trib had pictures - it was amazing," Stephanie said.

"She told me that she tried to take the cat with her when she climbed onto her roof with a hose. Butchie wouldn't go."

"Smart cat. What was Mrs. Creighton doing up there? Why wasn't she evacuated?"

Jenny hesitated, hating to talk about something she didn't really understand. "I guess we all need to know her psychological state to treat her. It was terrible. The fire department told her she was safe where she was. She didn't realize the danger until her neighbor's house caught fire. You might have heard about it on TV."

The other nurse shrugged. "Who has time to watch? Did she get trapped?"

"No, the firemen got her out in time. She said she didn't want to live if her house couldn't be saved. She was trying to put the fire out from her roof until the water pressure failed, then she just sat there using the chimney for support, waiting to die. We haven't told her much; the doctor wants us to wait until she's more stable. Burns are tricky - she's not out of the woods yet."

"What should we say if she asks about her house?"

"Just say you don't know. They're still checking the area and finding a few houses that survived the fire, even when everything around them burned. The doctor felt it might be easier on her if she believed her home was one of them."

"Does she believe you?"

"I don't know. She wants to hope. The problem is that I'm pretty sure the house is gone. I hate lying. Mostly, I'm hoping her daughter gets here soon. That should help. She seems so alone."

"Mrs. Creighton doesn't have much of a will to live right now. She's going to need a lot of care; I hope her daughter is up to it," Stephanie said.

* * *

Elaine woke when the first fingers of sun pried their way under her shade. Unable to get back to sleep, she dressed and looked in on Amanda. Crying sounds earlier in the night had brought Elaine running, only to encounter a locked door. The door was open now and Amanda slept, scrunched into a corner of the queen-size bed, rolled up in the comforter.

Elaine brewed coffee, then began to lay out some clothes and accessories for Amanda. Her gauzy, bright things made her feel romantic and sexy, but she remembered Amanda preferred tailored suits.

"Well! She has to have something to wear," Elaine said, adding a warm-up suit and a pair of jeans to the display on her bed.

While sipping coffee, Elaine bagged groceries from her pantry. If Jeff and Amanda couldn't use them, she would give them to other fire victims. Safeway was accepting food donations; it felt odd to plan to bring sacks back to the store.

She wanted badly to do something, to make some kind of sacrifice to the gods who had spared her home. Elaine had never considered the possibility of fire. Earthquakes didn't scare her - she was convinced she would have a chance to dig through the rubble for her treasures. But fire? Just a low pile of ashes left where a life used to be.

Hearing the shower, Elaine began to slice fruit and put out cereal for breakfast. Amanda appeared in a floral sundress; Elaine recognized it as resort wear, not the most comfortable thing on a foggy San Francisco morning.

"I have a sweater that would look great with that dress," she offered.

Amanda smiled. "I saw the fashion show in your room. It's really nice of you, but I couldn't possibly…"

"Of course you can," Elaine cut in. "I buy too much anyway. That's what comes of not having a life. Remember that." She smiled.

After they ate, Amanda dutifully tried on a few of the outfits. She posed in a dress that hung loosely to her calves.

"Okay, I get the message," Elaine laughed. "You're petite and I'm not. My colors wash you out. Want to go shopping?"

Amanda began to change back to her sundress. "Eventually, I'm sure I'll want to. I have to get some things for work."

Elaine gathered up her clothes. "Isn't there something I can do for you? I feel so…so…"

Amanda nodded. "I promise you I'll let you know. I just can't think about it yet."

Elaine reached for her and they hugged, awkwardly. Amanda pulled back first.

"The only thing I want to do now is find my mother. There's no answer at the house. There wouldn't be, I guess," she said.

Elaine smiled. "I know what we can do. Call Red Cross. They're maintaining a list of people - where they are staying and such. You should register with them too, when you're settled."

Amanda made no move to the phone, so Elaine dialed and then waited, tapping her fingers impatiently. She could hear the shuffling of paper and voices over the line calling out names. Finally, a voice returned. Elaine dialed another number quickly, murmuring her questions.

Elaine went to Amanda and took her hands. "Amanda, they've found your mother. She's at Herrick Hospital.

Wait… She's okay, I'm sure of it. They said that she had been asking for you; once she sees you, she'll be fine."

"What happened? Why is she in the hospital?"

"Your brave mother tried to save her house. She's been burned - painful, but the nurse said she will heal fully." Elaine hoped her voice didn't give a lie to the words. Ruth Creighton was not okay, but seeing Amanda had to help.

Elaine had always wondered about their relationship; she was close to <u>her</u> mother. The few times she had been with the two of them, the tension crackled. Elaine never understood. But despite the conflicts, she was sure Amanda loved her mother. This was going to be hard, harder than losing the house.

Elaine picked up her keys. "Come on - I'll drive you to Herrick."

*   *   *

Mrs. Creighton woke to the feeling of fingers gently brushing the hair from her eyes. She squinted. "Amanda?"

The hand was Elaine's; Amanda stood frozen, staring at the bandages.

"Help me sit up. Quick! I need to see my daughter," she cried.

Elaine adjusted the bed slowly, watching Mrs. Creighton's eyes puddle up as her shoulders rose.

"Amanda, are you okay?" she asked, extending her arms, then pulling back in pain.

"Mom, it's so awful. We lost everything… And look at you!"

Elaine backed away, leaving them alone. Amanda helped her mother to a drink of water, then stood quietly, as if unsure of what to do next.

"Are you settled somewhere yet?" Mrs. Creighton asked.

"Jeff has us in a horrible, poky motel. He doesn't even want to start looking for a place yet. All the good ones will be gone."

"You're clever, dear. You'll find something. Maybe you can locate a small cottage for me, for when I get out of here," she said.

"You know your house is gone?" Amanda was surprised; she hadn't been able to find out much.

"Yes." Mrs. Creighton's smile was faint. "They're trying to protect me, but I was there. I knew the house had already caught fire when they drove me away." Her eyelids fluttered; she was having difficulty keeping them open.

Amanda patted her shoulder gently, careful to touch only the unbandaged, unhurt area. "I'd better let you sleep. I'll be back soon."

Mrs. Creighton looked away. "Yes, do that dear. I'll sleep now." She closed her eyes.

Amanda left the room, stunned that she couldn't look to her mother for help. Jenny approached her.

"Mrs. Dunn. I wanted to talk to you about your mother's condition."

"Yes, yes. Tell me." They sat down in the sticky plastic chairs outside the nurse's station.

"Your mother is going to be okay, but she has to want to recover. Healing takes place first in the mind. We can only assist the process. You need to know that."

"But what can I do?" Amanda protested.

"She needs to know how much you love her. You're going to have to take care of her. Even when she's discharged, she can't go home alone."

"I guess I knew that," Amanda said.

"We're worried about her state of mind, Mrs. Dunn. Your mother made no move to leave her house, even after it was hopeless."

"What are you saying?"

"Just that I think she was giving up. She still might. You need to help her understand that you will willing to help her start over, to rebuild if she wants to. She's very frightened of that."

"But what can I do?"

"For now, find a place with room for her, then tell her about it. She needs to feel wanted. And try to find her cat. So many made it out, when most other animals didn't. I think that would help a lot."

Amanda sat, frozen, even after Jenny returned to her duties. Without realizing it, she had assumed she could rely on her mother, as she always had when things went wrong. She had clung to the thought all through the long flight from Maui. Mom will tell me what to do, she had thought.

"How am I going to go on?" she whispered. "Who is going to take care of me?"

29

CHAPTER 5

"Don't let your heart depend on things
That ornament life in a fleeting way!
He who possesses, let him learn to lose.
He who is fortunate, let him learn pain."

— Schiller

Jeff and Amanda joined the long line of cars backing up onto Highway 13. Ashes still smoldered and the smoke fogged the air, hiding the rescue workers from view.

Amanda settled into the bucket seat of her Honda CRX, wishing for the old bench-style seats that would give her a chance to get closer to Jeff. His voice had sounded brittle this morning when he called her at Elaine's; he wanted to check out their house. She put her hand on his neck, intending to massage it, but quickly pulled back. She didn't like the way his jaw had tightened at her touch.

"Damn them. What's taking so long?" Jeff's hands gripped the steering wheel until the whites of his knuckles threatened to break through the skin.

Amanda had been watching, while Jeff ground his teeth and inched up Hiller Road. "I don't think they're letting anyone up there."

"When did you become the big expert?" Jeff growled.

Instead of answering, she pointed to the road snaking up the hill above them. The only vehicles on it were rescue vans and fire trucks. A steady stream of cars doubled back down the road.

"No one's stopping me," Jeff said. "They may be able to talk other people into leaving, but not me. It's my property."

Amanda knew better than to argue with him. They continued to creep slowly up the road. Jeff turned off the air conditioning, so the engine wouldn't overheat.

A Berkeley policeman signaled Jeff to stop. He could see cars making wide U-turns ahead of him in an area defined by a row of police cars. "Can I see some ID, sir?" he asked.

"What for?" Jeff said brusquely.

"Sorry, sir. We need to identify those who live in the fire zone. There's a lot of people trying to get up here who don't belong."

Jeff passed over his whole wallet. The officer refused to take it. Yanking his license out of the plastic sheath, he tossed it out of the car, forcing the officer to grab for it. "So, convinced? I live here...err...I used to."

The policeman nodded, then returned his license with a small red card. "We can't let anyone into your area yet; we're not convinced the fire is fully contained. Come back in a day or two, or just listen to the radio. We'll broadcast an all-clear by neighborhood. Put this pass on your windshield and they'll let you through as soon as it's safe."

"Okay, Jeff, let's go back," Amanda said, patting his hand, trying to defuse his anger.

"No, damn it," Jeff roared. "I'm not turning around." He floored the accelerator, nearly knocking the policeman down as he passed. Driving on the soft earth on the shoulder, he squeezed past the police barricade.

"Jeff, no! We can't do this," Amanda protested. Oh, God! Don't we have enough trouble already?

"Who says? They let our house burn to the ground and now they have the gall to tell us to 'wait and see.' I'm going to see it now. The fire's out."

The officer recovered quickly and radioed up the hill for backup. Jeff found the road just around the turn blocked by a yellow fire truck. Another policeman jumped out and shouted into his megaphone, "Stop the car and get out slowly, hands on your head."

"Jeff, they're going to arrest us." Amanda was mortified.

Jeff paused, squinting through the windshield as he measured his options. He reached for the gun he had put in Amanda's glove compartment.

"No, Jeff. Do what they say," Amanda said. She unbuckled her seat belt with one hand, putting her foot on the glove box. "Don't make it any worse."

"How could it be worse?" Jeff said. He jumped out of the car and stood behind the door with his hands at his sides, defying the order. "Now, listen up. If you guys hadn't fucked up on Saturday putting out a stupid little brush fire, we would be driving home right now. Why do I have to wait for you to get your act together before I see what's left of my place?"

Amanda shrank back into her seat, shaking. Why can't he see? This isn't going to do any good. She wanted to go on a few more days, pretending it hadn't happened, or that there was a mistake and their house was safe. Once she saw it, her pretense would crumble.

Another fireman approached Jeff slowly, waving off the policemen who followed him, guns at the ready. "I'll handle it."

Jeff stiffened, keeping the officers and their guns in his sights.

"Let's talk. Okay?" The man's voice was quiet and friendly.

"What's your problem? I just want to see my house."

"I know. But we have a few things we have to do first."

"Like what?"

"Like find all the bodies," the officer snapped. "That's our number one priority. And we have to be sure the fire's out."

Amanda gasped. Bodies? Oh, God, it could have been her mother. It still could be some of their friends; there hadn't been time to check on everyone they knew. She was ready to turn the car around and drive straight to Montclair. He had to give this up.

Jeff started to speak, then ran towards the men, head down as if he intended to blast his way through. One grabbed his arm, twisting it up against his back, as he led him to his car.

"Ma'am? Do you have a license?"

Amanda nodded. The officer walked Jeff to the passenger side and waited for him to get in.

"Drive him home. Give your husband a chance to cool off."

Thank God. They weren't getting arrested. She put the car in reverse, avoiding Jeff's eyes. She knew how angry he would be at having been beaten down in front of her. Did he know how embarrassed she was by his behavior?

33

Amanda put on her sunglasses, putting further distance between them.

"Aren't you going to bust him?" one of the rescue workers asked.

"Naah. Leave him alone," the fireman said. "Stand in his shoes for a while. You might go ballistic too."

"Feeling guilty?" the worker challenged. "Afraid you didn't do all you could to put out the fire."

The fireman looked at his feet, then balled his fist. "We failed, damn it. Any time a fire kills people, we've failed. Yeah, we blew it. This isn't supposed to happen."

The men went back to their grim task, sifting through each home site, looking for the thing they hoped most not to find. But as the day wore on, the toll increased. The thousands who survived had no meaning to the workers in the face of the mounting fatalities.

*   *   *

Elaine unlocked her front door, surprised at the feeling of relief that came over her as she noted that all her belongings were safe. Setting her purse and briefcase down, she scanned her living room, using her brain as a camera, trying to capture the image. Elaine began a mental inventory, wondering how she would remember everything if she were to suddenly lose it.

"There are the cheap posters I framed in grad school," she began. "I wouldn't miss them much. And my aging stereo. Good excuse to get a new one." Elaine laughed. This wasn't so bad. "A new VCR, certainly. One with instructions in English this time."

Her laugh caught in her throat as she noticed the photo albums on the shelf just above her old record collection.

Elaine dropped to the floor and began pulling them out. How long had it been since she'd looked through them? They were her diary, the only record she had of her life. If her pictures burned, would her past shrivel into ashes with them?

A packet of negatives dropped out from between the pages of one book. Great! All the negatives neatly filed with the only prints I have. What was I thinking of?

Elaine set the albums aside and began to paw through the cardboard box she used as a file cabinet. She pulled out her renter's insurance, scanning it with real interest for the first time. On a bet, she couldn't have guessed what she was insured for, nor could she estimate how much more her belongings would cost to replace. She wouldn't have remembered the name of the insurance company; writing a check once a year hadn't embedded it in her mind. Behind the policy, she located the beginnings of an inventory. It was a list of replaceables, the things she had begun to realize she would rather replace. But what price for her first birthday pictures, the jeweled collar of her kitten, high school yearbooks bearing autographs and notes that could whisk her back to her teens in an instant?

Elaine choked. For a moment, she felt her loss as intensely as if it were real. What was wrong with her? It was Amanda who had been stripped bare, not her. She should be comforting others, not mourning phantom losses alone in her living room.

Filled with a sudden panic, Elaine decided that she had to plan for a disaster. Beginning on the back of a paper grocery bag - the only paper she could find - Elaine began a list of the things she didn't want to live without and how she could protect them. Tomorrow, I'll rent a camcorder, she told herself, but I can't wait for that now. Five minutes, perhaps only one trip with what I can carry. What would I choose?

She imagined grabbing up the things nearest to hand, staggering out of the apartment with her briefcase and her television. Panic clouds the mind, she thought. And the things you love, the things you most value are the ones you couldn't find at a time like that. You wouldn't even see them, because of how they have woven themselves into the fabric of your life.

It was oddly comforting to consolidate her irreplaceables near the front door, sorting out a few special things, all her negatives, keepsakes, and documents - things that should never have been left at home. She would rent a safe deposit box tomorrow. Five minutes. It seemed like no time at all.

CHAPTER 6

"What gives life its value you can find—and lose. But never possess. This holds good above all for 'the Truth about Life.'"
— Dag Hammarskjoeld

People dressed in early Salvation Army wandered in and out of the warehouse where FEMA had set up. It might have passed for a normal, even funky-looking gathering, except for the aching, staring eyes that echoed the anguish of a Keane painting.

The former neighbors waited patiently in each line to order copies of tax returns, apply for new driver's licenses, get coupons for furniture and clothes, or apply for low-cost loans. One-stop shopping, the volunteers had dubbed it, hoping that making things simple would help their clients get their lives back together. The creation of the center was one of the good things they had salvaged from the '89 earthquake.

Mere acquaintances greeted each other with bear hugs; the sight of a familiar face brought tears to many eyes. For those who lost everything, the center was a healing ground, a place to share the stories and lists of lost treasures non-survivors couldn't understand.

Amanda felt like congratulating herself for holding her emotions in check - unlike most of the others she saw - when she saw a black woman with close-cropped hair try to push herself and her wheelchair through the crowds without rolling over bare or sandal-clad toes. Amanda thought she knew her - a neighbor - one the Dunns had never taken the time to get to know, even though she had to be about the same age as Amanda.

Amanda rushed over, helping her roll to the place she wanted near the wall. She gave the woman a clumsy hug that encompassed the back of the wheelchair, enjoying the warmth of the spontaneous, uncharacteristic gesture.

"You made it - you're okay," Amanda stammered.

The woman smiled, returning the hug. "You, too," she said.

Amanda couldn't remember the woman's name, but she had seen her so many times, painfully wheeling herself up the single step into her house, or maneuvering the steep incline of Hiller Drive on crutches. She had heard mention of multiple sclerosis; Hiller Highlands wasn't the best place to live if you had mobility problems.

"I'm Pamela Macklin," the woman said, extending her hand.

"Amanda Dunn. We're neighbors, I think."

"Former neighbors, now," Pamela said, and they shared the laugh.

Pamela invited her to sit for a moment, so Amanda pulled up a chair. For a moment, the two stared at each other, unsure of what to say.

"What did you lose that you really, really hated?" Pamela began.

Their laughter bubbled up again. "There was this painting, or decoupage...something...that was given to us at our wedding," Amanda said. "Some old West thing…something that would look great in a ranch. And then, there's my china. My mother-in-law picked it out and I let her. It's so bad it actually looks better broken."

"I know exactly what you mean. I had piles of stuff my ex-husband left when he walked out. 'I'll be back to pick it up,' he said, but he never did. Serves him right," Pamela grinned. "Try and get it now."

Amanda felt immensely relieved at finding something worth laughing over. There were so many things she didn't have to worry about now, such as the cranky old appliances that had been incinerated for their obstinence. But looking at Pamela, she thought she saw pain behind the smile, and given Amanda's profession, she knew how much the separation must have cost her.

Amanda recovered her smile quickly. "Just think of going out and buying new clothes to fill new, empty closets. All our fashion mistakes erased; we can start fresh."

Pamela looked at her lap. "I've never really liked to shop."

Amanda thought she understood. Even to her, the task was a little daunting. What must it feel like to someone who couldn't stand to reach the high dress racks, who might have trouble moving through cramped stores. "Why don't we go together? I hate looking alone - I'm never sure how I look. And besides, the stores are offering some fabulous discounts. We can plunk ourselves down in a dressing room and let a personal shopper do all the work. And remember, we don't have to get it done in one day."

"I'd like that," Pamela said, her smile returning. "I really need to. Most of what I have was given to me by friends."

Amanda rolled her eyes skyward. "And such wonderful handouts, too! They meant well, I guess, but most of the stuff I've been offered is just dreadful. I can't imagine that my friends ever wore any of it, except to clean."

"And of course, we have to be <u>so</u> grateful," Pamela said, giggling. "You're right. Time to get some style back in our lives. Do you think our shopping trip could include a stop at an art store, so I can pick up some supplies. That's what I really miss right now."

"Are you an artist?" Amanda asked.

"Got to do something to pay the rent. No, I'm trivializing it. Art is what I love; I'm lucky that someone is willing to pay me to do it. I really want to get up into the hills. There's a stark beauty in the midst of all the destruction that I'd like to capture. Do you draw?"

"Not really, unless you count doodling on a legal pad. I'm a lawyer," Amanda said. "At least, I was before... I haven't seen my office, since it happened. Work seems so pointless now."

"This is a stopping point for us, I think," Pamela offered. "Nature making us revisit our assumptions."

Amanda nodded. "I like that thought."

They exchanged their temporary phone numbers and agreed on a time to meet for their shopping spree. Amanda had never made a friend that easily, nor had she ever let herself feel close to anyone that fast. It was Pamela, she decided. The openness, the lack of a protective shield drew people to her.

Scanning the room for Jeff, she began to notice other familiar faces. The joy of reuniting appeared to outweigh the pain, at least for this moment.

Amanda wished she could get caught up in the mood and use this opportunity to take a break from the painful itemization of lost treasures. The inventory of her worth was never far from her mind; reminders of her loss appeared everywhere.

"Have you checked the board yet?" A young man wearing a FEMA ID badge pointed to a wall crammed with pictures.

"What board?"

"Lost pets. They have pictures of pets they have recovered and you can list descriptions of ones the you're looking for. Check it out." The man moved on, pointing others to the list.

Amanda waded through the crowd and checked for her mother's cat. The pictures were sad - singed whiskers and feet, some animals with almost all their fur gone. Most of the recovered animals were cats. She wondered why. Were the dogs tied up, or did they get out with their owners? She shrugged. None of the scared souls looked anything like Butchie. Amanda made a promise to herself to check back every day or so. Butchie was kind of a mutt, but she knew how much the cat meant to her mother.

"Where have you been?" Jeff caught up with her, clutching a handful of forms and documents.

"Around. Seeing friends, neighbors," she replied.

"We don't know any of our neighbors," he said.

"I do now." Amanda caught another friendly eye and waved.

A tall, elderly man touched Jeff's arm gently. "You're okay, then. Excuse me, I'm sure you don't recognize me... maybe never noticed. I'm Peter Lewis. I used to watch you drive in every evening while I was walking Hamlet. I worried when I didn't see you or your lovely wife."

"We were away. Just got back," Jeff mumbled, wondering why he was being sought out.

"All of us are what's left of our neighborhood," Peter said. "We have to stick together and rebuild."

Jeff didn't respond, hoping the old man would take the hint and find someone else.

"Perhaps it's too soon for you to think about it." Peter extracted a crumpled, hand-typed card from his pocket. "We're forming Phoenix neighborhood groups."

"Phoenix?"

"Remember? The mythical bird rising from its own ashes? We liked the symbolism of it and the hope."

"How do you expect anyone to find time for this?"

"We thought that together, neighborhoods could actually rebuild faster. I think it will be worth the investment in time. Join us, when you're ready."

Jeff took the card, crumpling it in his hand. Find no wastebasket nearby, he surprised himself by smoothing it out and tucking it into his wallet. He wasn't a joiner, but maybe a group like that <u>would</u> get the job rolling faster. Government red tape was likely to snarl up the works before anyone would be allowed to clear their foundations.

Neighbor. The word reminded Jeff of the small Illinois town he grew up in, where each new family was greeted with a covered dish offering or home-canned goods. He knew his neighbors then and they helped each other through the February ice storms and occasional tornado. Not much need for neighbors in California, he had always thought. And the closeness could be intrusive, he remembered, thinking of his teen years. He didn't want people depending on him, leaning. But perhaps now...

No. Committees always made things worse. Even as a manager, Jeff hated delegating important work; he never gave an assignment to a group, when on talented employee could manage it alone. The accident of their being neighbors meant nothing.

But they still all had the same work to do now, the same hoops to jump through, he told himself. It wouldn't help him any to rebuild if he had to live amid empty lots filled with burned garbage. The Dunns had a stake in getting the neighborhood back.

Thinking of the remnants of brick chimneys, twisted signs and concrete slabs as a neighborhood made Jeff laugh until the tears globbed up in his eyes. In his private, hysterical fit, Jeff didn't care which - tears or laughter - came first.

CHAPTER 7

"I cannot but remember such things
That were most precious to me."
— Shakespeare

Amanda found it difficult to sit in the passenger seat of her car and not look at anything, to block out the destruction on both sides of Highway 13. She closed her eyes, but the images of charred, limbless eucalyptus trees seemed embedded on the inside of her eyelids. She looked at her husband with resentment - all he had to do was stare at the gray tarmac and white lines. He didn't have to see.

Jeff took the turn onto Tunnel Road hard, making the tires of the small car squeal. My car, Amanda thought. You wouldn't have done that to your Mercedes. Or maybe he would have. Jeff was careless of his possessions, expecting them to survive his abuse unharmed. Amanda pushed that thought aside. DANGEROUS ROAD AHEAD.

The line of houses that guarded the hilltop was gone, leaving only a single house frame, like a gate to nowhere. It reminded her of the devastation of Hurricane Hugo, but here the ground was blackened with soot and ash, not leaves and water. Black-barked, nearly dead trees rose up in defiance of the reports of their demise. Protected in their air-conditioned cocoon, Amanda and Jeff were spared the singed-hair, smoldering plastic smells outside. The view was so much like the wreckage wreaked by any natural disaster, but this was where she had lived. Easier to pretend that the alien landscape was alien because it wasn't her home.

Winding up Hiller Road, Jeff began to take the turns more slowly, trying to avoid the abandoned cars and uncleared fire debris on the narrow, steep road. Where condos had clustered tightly together, there was only a clearing.

"I can see the shadows of the houses that were once here," Amanda said, not meaning to speak the words aloud, unaware of how they gave voice to her desire.

Jeff nodded, easing up on the accelerator. He looked at her and in that moment, she sensed their shared desperation and anger.

"How can we start over?" Jeff asked. The question hung in the air, and Amanda felt she could hear an echo of it from the vacant lots. How could anyone?

"I can't remember where anything was." Jeff twisted in his seat, looking for a landmark.

Amanda covered his hand with hers.

"It's gone. Forever. How can we rebuild it?" Jeff growled.

The tires of the CRX crunched down on the edge of their felled street sign as they turned up Schooner Hill.

"Look, Jeff." Amanda pointed to a neighbor, smeared with soot, digging through the rubble. "What can they hope to find?"

"I have no idea," Jeff said. He continued to stare only at the road, though their curve of the street was mostly cleared of debris.

"Do we know those people?" Amanda gestured frantically at a couple digging on a lot two away from theirs. "I thought two old ladies lived there. That's not their car!"

"Damn it. I was afraid of this." Jeff blared the horn at the couple. "They're looters. A bunch of goddamn ghouls. So much for the security we were promised." He fumbled in the glove box, then slammed it shut, letting maps and car manuals spill out.

"Where's the gun I gave you?"

Amanda frowned. "I took it out. I knew I couldn't use it."

"What in hell are we supposed to do?"

Amanda looked pointedly at his cell phone, but remained silent, knowing how he hated advice.

Jeff drove the car up the lip of the sidewalk, blasting his horn continuously at the looters. "Get lost, assholes!"

The young couple grabbed their green plastic garbage bags and one scurried back to the dented copper station wagon.

"Looters should be shot!" Jeff shouted.

"What business is it of yours?" the man asked, putting down the bag.

"It's everyone's business to keep thieves out of the neighborhood."

The sweating man took a step towards Jeff, then stopped. "Not that I'm answerable to you, but my mother lived here." He twisted the end of the sack into a knot, slowly cinching it in. "She died." He hoisted the bag, then joined his wife in the car.

Amanda found a scream lodged in her own throat, trapped by years of practice. She never swore. What would she have yelled if her vocal chords hadn't clamped down?

Jeff reversed the gears, then pulled back onto the road, spewing ashes. He drew up in front of 161, their home. Only the numbers painted on the broken curb marked the space.

"Look, honey. I'm sorry," he began. "I just couldn't believe the nerve… What a story!"

"It's okay," Amanda said, taking his hand. "I think for a moment, I wanted to shoot them, too."

"Some protection these passes are," Jeff said, crumpling the red card. "Every looky-loo and tramp will be up here before we've had a chance."

"I never realized what it would be like to watch people slow down before an accident when I was the one trapped in the car," Amanda said. "I feel invaded. It's like they take pleasure in seeing this, because it isn't them." She stayed in her seat, staring at her hands.

Jeff opened the car door for her - he never did that, but then, she had never wanted him to - then pulled her close for a moment. "There's a lot of scum out there."

His words comforted her and in them, Amanda heard all the other things he couldn't say. They were together in this, even if they had nothing else. That alone might give her the strength to get through it. Arms around each other's waist, they turned to look at their enlarged view, extending expansively from the Alameda Naval Air Station to Mt. Tamalpais. The arch of the Golden Gate bridge gleamed, contrasting with the duller gray of the Bay Bridge. Without the occasional chimney looming out of the dirt, it would have been hard to imagine that houses had ever been there. Once the debris was cleared, the hilly ground would look more like a new development than a ruin.

"Oh, God!" Jeff's voice sounded strangled.

"What is it?"

"My car."

Together, they looked at the stripped-to-bare-metal hulk sitting where their garage used to be. Amanda was surprised he recognized it as his; the elegant blue paint and plush leather seats were only a memory.

"I'm sorry," Amanda said. She imagined that they would respond differently to their losses, but she never dreamed that something like a car would mean so much to him.

"That car - I bought it when I made vice-president. It was my first indulgence, my first tangible proof of what I had accomplished."

Amanda gripped his hand, trying to let him know that she understood, even though she didn't.

"What now?" Jeff asked.

"Let's look. Maybe we can find something worth keeping," Amanda said. "We should go to Mom's too and look for her."

She hoped they would find some surviving treasure of Jeff's, but then, what particular thing did he hold dear? For herself, she remembered photo albums, old cards and letters from boyfriends. Flowers she had pressed in books, the quilt her grandmother had pieced together for her, the beaded bracelet she had made at Girl Scout camp... So much, so many precious mementos that marked the passage of her life. Could this fire have obliterated her past?

What about Jeff? They could buy him another car - a Mercedes if he wanted one - that was easy. It wouldn't be the same, but she couldn't see how it would matter, once he drove the new one a few times. His tools and gun collection? They could probably replace them too.

Amanda simply couldn't think of a thing he owned that was irreplaceable. Not even the wedding pictures. That reminded her of Jeff's resentment when he got the bill from the photographer. As much as she had liked the studio prints, she couldn't remember looking at them after the wedding.

"We have to start making lists for the insurance," Jeff said.

"Do we have to do it now?" Amanda asked. "I can't think. At this moment, I can't even visualize our living room, let alone remember what was in it."

"The sooner the better. We want to get at the head of the line with the adjuster. Look at this," Jeff gestured at the barren hills. "Everyone is going to be rushing in, trying to get their claim filed."

Amanda stared at the lot. Why should they have to make a list when it was clear that everything was gone? Wouldn't the insurance company just give them the full amount of their policy?

She caught sight of their mailbox, lying on its side in the dirt, a fallen warrior. Out of habit, Amanda pulled open the door. The box was empty even of ashes, reminding her that they had put a hold on their mail. Picking it up was just another task to add to the list.

"Nothing left." Jeff shook his head, his eyes never leaving the charred remains of their home, as if by staring, he could make the house reappear. Amanda ran to him and they clung together tightly, trying to save the other from drowning in the panic and despair.

"I didn't know it would be like this," Amanda said, slowly. She had seen it burn, had heard the stories, but could not envision the obliteration of her home. This was real. The rawness of the burned-down-to-the-metal

49

Mercedes skeleton rasped inside her. Amanda paced out the lot, trying to imagine where their bedroom, once a large part of the second floor, would have ended up. She knelt and began to sift through the ashes, pulling up twisted and melted items whose shape was irretrievably altered.

"Honey, look!" Jeff held up a blackened revolver, smiling broadly. She didn't recognize it, but she knew he would. He had started his search in his study, a place she knew only on the infrequent occasions when she had to go in to clean. "There's probably lots of stuff here. We just have to look," Jeff said.

Amanda continued to run her fingers through the dirt and ash until she too located a treasure - a chunky bracelet of coral - black coral now - that Jeff had bought on their first Hawaiian vacation. She could see again the ancient Hawaiian who had sold it to them from his pushcart in Waikiki. Despite Jeff's best bargaining technique, the vendor's gap-toothed smile told them who ended up with the better part of the deal. It was the first piece of jewelry Jeff had given her, back when their relationship was new and untried.

Amanda cleared a spot on the low brick wall that bordered their driveway and carefully set the bracelet down. Jeff added a handful of pictures that had survived under an overturned metal tray. They stopped to examine each one.

Amanda smiled at the brownish, scallop-edged picture of her mother cradling a blanket-wrapped bundle. Another showed a 6-year old Jeff, proudly dragging a red wagon full of leaves behind him. She remembered his stories of early business savvy; Jeff could always find a way to make money. Each picture reminded her of another story, another memory of childhood. Just a few weeks before, her mother had presented her with some well-preserved pictures, inspiring Amanda to put a special album together. It would be a thin album now, she mused.

Several feet away, she spotted their first edition copy of "Gone With the Wind." Rereading this book in the tub while sipping a chilled glass of white wine was always a special treat. It felt like a gift that the book had survived. As she touched the binding, the "book" crumbled to dust. Amanda watched as the fragments scattered, caught in an air current. She choked on the dust, wishing she had brought water. Her throat hurt, ravaged by smoke and ash.

Settling back down in the area she thought might have been her walk-in closet after the fire dropped the second story down on the first, Amanda began to sift again. There was no hope of finding unburned clothes, but maybe a buckle or some jewelry had survived. She had forgotten their small wall safe until she bumped her knee against it. The knee stung, but she barely noticed it.

"Jeff! The safe!" Even though the exterior showed fire damage, she still believed something inside would have survived. Struggling, they lifted the squat box to the hatchback of their car.

"We'll get it hacked open by a professional," Jeff said. "My coins are in there."

And my jewelry, Amanda thought. She found herself more interested in a favorite pair of Amalfi shoes she found crushed under the safe when the walls collapsed. Perching one on her fingertips, she considered if it might be salvageable, then laid the pair carefully next to her other finds. Jeff grinned, shaking his head at the wrecked shoes she would probably never wear.

To their surprise, a small set of china quail chicks and a mother hen appeared, dirty, but unbroken, from the area that might have been the kitchen. Another memento. She took a moment to recall where and why she had bought them. A country store in Bird In Hand, Pennsylvania, when they did the Amish tour on their bikes. Amanda thought she might be pregnant and bought the set to commemorate the beginning of their family. She patted her too-flat stomach, remembering the cramps that ended her hope.

All those years of dusting and until today, she hadn't remembered their origin. Just the kind of thing that didn't merit a mention on an insurance list, but so precious, remembering. Tears ran freely down her face, cleaning tracks in the soot. Amanda noticed wetness in Jeff's eyes. Jeff took her hand and drew her to the back of their lot. Poking through blackened dirt, an aster defied the destruction with its brave color. More than anything else they had found, this single sign of life elated her. If it could push itself up through the ashes... if a flower could start over...

Amanda didn't understand the intensity of the joy she felt on what had to be the worst day of her life. She didn't question the gift. It was enough just having this moment.

CHAPTER 8

"He who possesses most must be most afraid of loss."
— Leonardo DaVinci

Leaning on her crutches, Pamela surveyed the charred, concrete foundation of her house, marked only by a tall tombstone-like remnant of her chimney. With her artist's eye, she recreated the structure, room by room, and for a moment in time, the image flickered into focus. As it faded, a sob choked her. Pamela had always believed that what could be imagined was more than halfway to being real. Never before had it occurred to her how easily the dream could be obliterated.

Cursing her unstable legs, she guided herself carefully to the spot where her studio would have been. The first night, Pamela just felt happy to be alive; the loss of her art work hadn't really touched her. She couldn't think about it, let alone accept it. Knowing how slim the chance was, she still hoped that at least one of her small sculptures had survived. Stone shouldn't burn. The paintings would only live in her memory as long as she was able to see them there; Pamela imagined the colors of the oils shooting through the flames, making a dramatic, but ephemeral glow before their substance became fuel. For a moment, the thought gave her pleasure, until she saw the analogy to fireworks - beautiful for a moment, but ultimately of no value. Pamela was her art - the M.S. meant that she would never be able to recreate most of this. Sinking to her knees, she cried, mourning the loss of herself much more than of her art.

The point of her crutch caught on a rough spot in the floor. She knelt to pick up a carved hand, wrought from river stone. A few steps ahead, she could see where the walls had fallen over her workbench. Nothing but a crane could lift the heavy blocks. None of her delicate stone-work could have survived such abuse.

Starting over. How many times did a person have to begin again, and from where was she to draw the resolve to do it? Many of her beginnings had been joyous - her graduations, wedding, the day she thought she was finally pregnant - but those days were tucked away in a past that had perhaps happened to someone else. Or to herself in another lifetime.

The recent ones - the ones that marked their passing with peculiar aches in a different part of her body - had all been hard. The day she found out she had multiple sclerosis, the horror of it had been too large to understand. With the awful words, her doctor had interjected hope, telling her of the research that was already netting positive results in others. But for Pamela, the loss of control of her hands and the visual disturbances were worse than a death sentence. Who was Pamela Macklin if she could no longer be an artist?

But with Brian's help, she knew she could keep going. She could find a way to create. At first, he had been as sympathetic and as loving as she had needed. Until the day he left. She remembered how he wouldn't meet her eyes, the furtive way he moved to the door, carrying a duffel bag in his hand.

"It isn't you, Pamela," he said. "It's me. I'm not good enough - not strong enough."

She always wondered who he had met. Better always to believe that he had left her for someone else than to imagine her illness had repulsed him. That she had proved too needy for him. But why shouldn't her M.S. repulse him, when she could barely stand to look at herself in the mirror on the bad days?

She remembered. Pamela Green Macklin, artist, activist, loner until she fell in love for the first and only time in her life. Handsome Brian, funny, smart, charming Brian.

Pamela cried when he left, cried at the diagnosis; she had to scrape the bottom of her tear ducts to find anything left to shed for her house and her art. She tried to convince herself that the heap of ashes proved that she could create and would again, but the words rang hollow inside her head. Not for the first time since the diagnosis, Pamela found she was tempted to play the role life had assigned her - that of an invalid whose sole accomplishment each day was to survive. Somehow, it had never been enough. The steel spine she inherited from her ancestors wouldn't allow her to admit defeat. She willed it to bear her up through the crisis.

The destruction of the house began with Brian's leaving; the fire only made it real. Whatever home she made for herself now she would carry within her.

Making a conscious effort to detach herself from the scene, Pamela began to see the interplay of light and shadow, the colors emerging from charred bricks and splintered trees. Returning to her car, she took out a pad of paper and some charcoal. Bracing her right hand with a wrist splint, Pamela began to sketch the scene, seeing nature's anger in the ashes and her forgiveness in the small shoots of plants already forcing themselves up between the shattered concrete blocks.

* * *

"Have we ever met this guy?" Jeff asked, as they sat outside the office of their insurance agent. He squirmed in his borrowed suit.

"We must have...when we got the policy... Didn't we?" Amanda said. It might have been easier if they had some kind of relationship with the man. But who did? Amanda didn't remember anything about their insurance policy; had she and Jeff ever talked about it? How much could they count on to rebuild?

"Are you the Dunns?" the agent asked brusquely, leaning his head out the door. His black hair was slicked back - a fashion statement or too many days without washing. A gold pinkie ring dominated his hand; his belly spilled over his pants, straining at the buttons of his shiny suit.

The agent disappeared. Amanda and Jeff rose to follow him in. Not a good start, Amanda thought.

"You've probably been swamped with claims this week," she began, hoping to placate him.

"It's always something. Earthquake, fire - not much difference to me," he said, leafing through their file.

Amanda whispered to Jeff, taking his hand to draw him close. "What's his name?" she asked.

Jeff raised his eyebrows instead of shrugging. "Beats me."

Amanda shuddered.   Surely this would get off to a better start if they could address him by name.   She craned her neck trying to read his business cards upside down; he laid their file down on top of as much of his desk as possible, clearly annoyed at her attempts to snoop.

"I've looked your policy over," the agent began.   "I don't know what you were expecting…"

Amanda gulped.   "We've started a list of our belongings.   They said down at Red Cross that it would help."

The agent grimaced.   "Most people's personal stuff isn't worth the paper to jot it down, but you have to start somewhere."   He examined a worksheet as if to estimate all over again their net worth.   "I can offer you two-twenty-five max for the house and up to another sixty thou on personal property, provided you can document your losses. Lists are one thing; ownership papers are better."

Amanda and Jeff stared at each other.   The house cost them $225,000 ten years ago.   Surely it would cost more now, with labor higher and wood so much more expensive. Amanda wondered how she would document their art collection, her jewelry.   What kind of proof did he need?

Jeff started to rise from his seat, leg muscles tense under the ill-fitting pants.   "That's not enough to rebuild our house.   No way."

"It's a start," the agent replied.   "And it's all you paid for."   He looked at his watch, then closed the file and sat back.

"Like hell! We've paid high premiums for replacement value for years.   What the fuck are you talking about?" Jeff stood, leaning over the desk to spit his words at the bland, shiny face of the insurance agent.

"It wasn't guaranteed full replacement value. That is the only option where we will rebuild your house as it was, if its value has increased. I believe I mentioned that at the time I drew up your policy. You weren't interested."

"I wasn't? Since you're such a fucking expert, tell me why I didn't go for it?"

"Too expensive. I believe those were your words," the agent said. His tone was bland, unreactive.

What was the difference between replacement value and guaranteed replacement, Amanda wondered. She didn't believe the agent had ever made that clear. How many others were getting taken advantage of by this clause, if it even existed?

She tugged gently at Jeff's jacket, then whispered in his ear. "We can't do anything here; he won't listen to us. Maybe we should get a lawyer."

Jeff ignored her. "You're picking nits here," Jeff said. "Guaranteed…full…replacement is replacement."

With a flourish, the agent flung a legal document at them. "Section 221-C. Check the small print. 'This policy reflects replacement value only up to the stated policy limits.' That's two-twenty-five."

"No. That's bullshit." Jeff grabbed the policy and tore it in half. "Here. Eat this."

Amanda wanted to applaud; she would have slunk out of there, maybe calling a lawyer, maybe just giving up. She felt immense gratitude that Jeff would stand up for them. Jeff took her arm and led her to the door.

"You haven't heard the last of me," he said. "If I have to, I'll take you to court." Amanda smiled when Jeff allowed himself the luxury of slamming the outer door.

She whispered 'I love you' as Jeff opened the car door for her, receiving a small smile in response.

"That was round one, Amanda. Those adjusters figure we're stupid, or just too upset to fight." He looked straight into her eyes. "Amanda, next time, I go alone. Anyone could see you'd cave in and sign. You're just a liability in this kind of situation."

* * *

Jeff drove to the airport alone, leaving Amanda at home trying to arrange another room at their motel. They still hadn't found an apartment; Jeff wasn't ready. Getting an apartment would force them to start replacing their possessions. Jeff needed more time to consider what he wanted. It might be a good opportunity to move to a higher level, a better grade of furniture and stereo equipment. He had earned it.

As excited as he was about seeing his daughter again, he was equally concerned about her effect on Amanda. War usually broke out within the first few hours of a visit; he wished they had something in common, something that would bring them together. Like Leslie and I have.

Jeff smiled remembering all her teenage years when she had no time for him, and nothing to say. Picking up golf to impress a boyfriend the summer after high school graduation, she discovered a love for the game. Jeff didn't care how she got started; it was the beginning of a friendship for them, one that improved with every stroke.

His smile faded, as he remembered his last words to Amanda when he left the house. With her mother, the house, everything - could she handle a temperamental stepdaughter too?

"If you don't want to go back to work yet, don't," Jeff had said. "You can always find something else."

Amanda's eyes flashed angrily. "Do you have any idea how hard I worked to get where I am?"

"And where are you, <u>exactly</u>?" Jeff regretted the words immediately. He knew how much her failure to make partner hurt her.

"No matter how much I do, it's never enough. If you wanted a stay-at-home wife, you should have stayed with Sheila. I have a career." She stomped out of the room.

Jeff shook his head, remembering. Everything he said lately set her off. They were like flint and tinder, sparking up the smoldering dirt around them. Having Leslie here would probably make things worse, but how could he tell her not to come?

"Dad!" Leslie waved a neatly manicured hand, flipping her silk scarf back around her neck with practiced flair.

She could have been a model, Jeff thought. He smiled, thinking that a career in art was the second to last thing he would have picked for her.

Leslie looked into the car, as she tossed her garment bag into the trunk. "So, where's the bitch?"

Jeff groaned. "Don't start. Please."

"Sorry." Leslie tossed the word off casually. "Just thought she might be here to do the family thing."

"She's trying to arrange a room. We haven't found an apartment yet. Can't you cut her some slack?"

"As much as she cuts me. Why did you marry her? I could understand sex, but…"

Jeff's hand flung out, nearly slapping her. He pulled it back, shaking. "Why the hell did you come?"

Leslie stared at her lap. "I thought you needed me."

"What for? To start more trouble with Amanda?"

Leslie reached for her father's hand, then kissed him on both cheeks. "I'll try, Dad. You know I will." Out of long habit, Leslie crossed her fingers as she spoke, hiding them under her pleated skirt.

Jeff shook his head. He could see that Leslie was gearing up for a campaign against Amanda, despite her promises. The sweet, sad smile on her face didn't fool him. They would have to find something to rent - sharing a motel room would never work.

Denise P. Kalm

CHAPTER 9

"He knows not his own strength that hath not met adversity."
— Ben Jonson

Amanda stepped into the law offices of Jones, Kaplan and watched while the cyclone of activity whirled past her. Before the fire, she would have rushed into it, exhilarated by the pace. Today, it just made her tired, as tired as she looked. Extra minutes at the mirror, dabbing at her face with cover-up, hadn't helped to hide the hollows in her cheeks or the dark circles under her eyes. Amanda's hand shook as she tried to draw a straight line with the eyeliner.

Leslie's arrival had driven her from the relative sanctuary of their motel room, but returning to work failed to quiet the anxiety she felt since the fire. Noises made her jump. People pressed too close to her; she felt trapped by their odors, their sounds, the feel of their eyes on her. Of the two priorities, Amanda decided that the familiarity of work would be more soothing than fighting the hordes to land an apartment at a reasonable rate. Last night, she had convinced herself that she could work on auto-pilot, but today, it didn't seem possible. She had stepped out of line, off the conveyor belt, and now, her co-workers were too far ahead, uncatchable.

Amanda hurried past the secretaries, hoping to reach her office unnoticed.

"Mrs. Dunn," a voice called out.

Damn. Amanda turned to see a young, overly-pierced secretary waving a sheaf of phone messages at her.

"We didn't know where to reach you," she said. "Mr. Jones has been calling down here every day. He wants to speak with you."

No welcome, just irritation at her unavailability. She gave one last glance into her silent office, needing badly to close herself into her comfortable cocoon, just to sit quietly for a moment. She had to run the gauntlet of eyes - secretaries and associates - on her march to the senior partner's office. A summons was generally a death sentence; most who had taken that walk had not returned.

"Welcome back," Henry Jones greeted her with a frosty smile, devoid of welcome.

Amanda realized she didn't know what to say, hadn't prepared for this confrontation. "I'm sorry I've been out of touch... So much to do... We don't even have a place to live yet. Or a phone number. I should have left something."

She looked for sympathy or at least understanding in his eyes. The old Amanda would have faced him down, would have forced him to take the initiative. She hated ceding control so readily.

"Work has been piling up in your absence."

Absence. Did she need a note from home to explain herself?

"Everyone carries their own caseload here. Others have had to pick up your clients." Jones shuffled paper while he talked, not even stopping to peer at her over his glasses.

"I'm hoping to be back at work full time very soon," Amanda offered, hoping that it was enough, hoping that she would be able to manage it. His throat clearing told her that he expected the same 80-plus weekly hours out of her that she had been happy to put in before the fire. A zillion years ago, when her only dream was to make partner. Another life, a different Amanda.

She wanted to fill the silence with something, apologies, explanations, anything, but the commitment he demanded of her.

"Are you here to put in billable hours today?" he said, after pausing long enough to make her think she might have been dismissed.

Amanda shook her head. Her first intention this morning had been to throw herself at her job, but now, she couldn't imagine how she could begin. "I needed some papers, for the insurance..."

"Yes?"

"And to check on anything really pressing," she said, caving in to the expression on his face.

"The others are capable of handling your work if you can't do it," Jones said. "In fact, glad of the chance to prove themselves."

The audience was over. Amanda hated the thought of scrounging for clients again, bribing secretaries to throw new cases her way, taking on the high profile pro bono work to impress the partners, all the politics that had been a part of her life since she had joined the firm. But the unspoken "or else" made her position clear. This was the way of life with an associate - keep climbing, keeping making money or you're gone.

But she hadn't been fired, yet. She swallowed her anger, fighting to keep herself moving forward, but struggling with the mad desire to rush into his office again. She could hear the words she wanted to say - you give people time off to have babies, you let Hughes work from home all those weeks, when his back went out, but when my life is destroyed, nothing.

But counselor, she argued with herself, Hughes is a partner. And no woman who took more an a week off to have a baby had ever made partner. When she joined this competitive firm, she knew they hired more than twice the number of associates needed. Jones claimed they would thrive on the competition, and at one time, Amanda had. The odds never scared her; she had never considered they applied to her.

Amanda maintained her courtroom poise as she entered her small office and closed the door. Her leather chair beckoned; she curled up in it, weeping softly. The heavy walls of law books and opinions closed in on her, a padded trap. You are a lawyer, the walls seemed to say. If not that, then who are you?

Amanda reminded herself of the faceless ones, the lawyers who refused to put in long hours, never shorted sleep or their families. The firm made the policy clear - we are your priority. We are your life. Be an automaton, or go. It wasn't personal; it wasn't about her.

But I can't afford to lose this job, she thought. We need money - lots of it - but at the very least, we have to have something for the day-to-day expenses. Jeff and Amanda never saved much of their large incomes, preferring to enjoy the purchases of a moment, all of which were now gone. Until the insurance came through - if it ever did - they would have to buy groceries, put down a deposit on an apartment, try to get back to a normal life. They were both on salary, but she would have to start earning it again. How?

Amanda knew that she had little in reserve to offer her grieving clients - people who needed her support and caring during painful divorces and child custody battles. The job took so much out of her, even on a good day.

She envied Jeff, who had been able to return to work immediately. Picking up the reins of his old life, he buried himself in paperwork and meetings; losing himself in work helped him. It's like he has an "off" switch on his emotions. Why can't I turn mine off?

Amanda grabbed a few case files, her mail and phone messages, and left. Maybe in the home she had yet to find, she could get some work done. The office sucked energy from her. Waiting until the cacophony of phones and printers reached a peak, she slipped out of her office, using the fire stairs to avoid any further contact.

*   *   *

Pamela rolled her chair out the door of the realty office, holding a sheaf of listings. "If we owned rental property, today would be a field day," she said. "I can't believe the prices they're charging; this isn't San Francisco."

Amanda shook her head. "What can we do about it? Only Berkeley has rent control."

"Some of these listings <u>are</u> Berkeley." Pamela handed a few pages to Amanda. "Isn't this illegal?"

"Probably. But while we take action against the worst goudgers, the rest of the places will be gone. We don't have much choice."

"Want to check out a few of these together?" Pamela suggested.

"Maybe we should shop first," Amanda said, looking at the two of them. Pamela was wearing an over-sized runner's tee-shirt over a pair of sooty jeans. Amanda noticed a tear in the light dress she wore - the sweater covered it, barely.

"There's nothing they haven't seen before," Pamela said. "Besides, no one else is trying to look right now. We can't hide the fact that we really need a place."

They started in Oakland, wanting to be as close to their old lives as possible, but the dirty air and charred trees depressed them too much. Like living in a war zone, Amanda commented, and Pamela agreed. The clearer air of Orinda looked appealing and the commute for the Dunns would only be slightly longer.

The pair presented themselves at the rental office, flustering the lavendar-coiffed secretary at the desk. "Ah, yes... We have some vacancies, but only in our more expensive units." She looked down her pinched nose at Pamela, trying to smile at Amanda at the same time.

Angered, Amanda grabbed Pamela's chair and wheeled her into the parking lot. "Does this happen often?"

Pamela shrugged. "You get used to it. Either it's my color or my handicap."

"I don't want to live in a place that would treat you like that," Amanda said, not wanting to be separated from her new friend.

"No." Pamela's voice rang out. "You can't take on my problems; you need a place too. I can bunk with my aunt a while longer. It's not bad and her house is all on one level. Much easier for me."

"What are you saying?"

"It was a bad idea, looking together. I didn't think…maybe hoped that it would be different, but it isn't. This is how things are," Pamela said.

Have I been living in this world, Amanda wondered? Do people still act like that? She and Jeff had always believed in equal rights and they weren't a bit racist. Were they?

As she helped Pamela into her car, Amanda realized that in some ways, she had been kidding herself. Easy to pretend to be open-minded if you never had to make good on the promise. Pamela was her first black friend; had it not been for the fire, they would never have spoken. She had Asian friends in college, colleagues really. She couldn't remember ever going out to dinner or a movie with one of them, nor had she ever considered someone of a different race as a partner.

"I'm sorry," she said, not knowing what else to say.

"Amanda, this is the world. It's getting better, but I can't imagine people will ever be able to view everyone as an equal. They need to feel superior, need to keep their distance. I'd be lying if I said I didn't mind. I do. But I can't change it."

Amanda squeezed Pamela's hand, then drove her home, helping her roll the short distance to the house. She returned to Orinda, signing a lease for the first apartment she saw, mindless of the cost. She needed a roof. Later, she could worry about making it a home. Her life felt very temporary, as if nothing she did made any permanent difference. Only fire changes things, she thought.

Amanda drove to Montclair, hoping to find that the food she had left for her mother's cat had been eaten. She had put out a bowl on the house site, near where the fireplace used to be. Butchie liked curling up next to the familiar hearth. Maybe he still would. She had a sack with her containing the dry Purina pellets that were a staple of his diet, as well as several cans of the more tempting wet food he liked.

The small bowl was empty. Amanda realized that she had no way of knowing who or what had eaten it, but she hoped. Butchie would try to come back - she was sure of it. Where else could he go? The memories drew them back, people and animals alike. At first, it seemed strange that people would sit on their property in lawn chairs, looking at nothing. Now, Amanda thought she understood.

In the fading afternoon light, Amanda ran her fingers through the dirt again, still hoping to find an unburned something to give her mother. She tried each time she left food for the cat, unable to believe that the fire could destroy everything.

This time, her nail caught on something and tore. She unearthed a small metal box, whose carved silver surface had melted into a smear. Using a bit of scrap metal, Amanda managed to pry it open. Two rings fell out - her mother's wedding rings, now too small for her arthritis-swollen fingers. The gold held its shape, but the diamonds were loose; she would have to take them to be repaired. She clutched the rings tightly, afraid to lose one of the tiny chips. They reminded her of the faded wedding pictures she had once loved to pore over. Her parents' wedding had been very traditional. When she expressed a twinge of envy - Jeff and she had eloped to Tahoe, leaving barely enough time for her to buy a new suit - her mother reminded her that it hadn't been a gala.

"Just our friends and families. Everyone brought something and my favorite aunt, Mary, made the wedding cake," Mrs. Creighton told her, smiling at the memory.

Denise P. Kalm

Looking at the rings, Amanda realized how much she wanted memories like these. The Dunn's wedding was little more than a furtive weekend getaway; they hadn't shared the moment with anyone.

Her father died a few years ago. "His heart just gave out," her mother had said. His death should have brought mother and daughter closer, but it hadn't. Ruth Creighton moved from grief into a frenzy of redecoration. The house completed, she found a circle of friends - other widows - and plunged into a more active life. Amanda wanted the other mother back - the one who worried over her. The one who sat home quietly, who made wonderful, elaborate dinners.

The one who always seemed to know the answers to every problem.

Knowing that the mother she wanted was gone long before, Amanda couldn't help trying to find her in the house site and in the body of the badly burned woman at Herrick Hospital.

* * *

Later, trying to sleep next to a snoring Jeff, Amanda began thinking about how much they would need in their new place. She rose quietly, slipping out to the nearest Safeway, where she filled a cart with cleaning supplies, staples, like spices and flour, and enough produce for several feasts.

The bleary eyes of the checker only acknowledged the quantity she laid on the moving belt. Few others shopped the stores at 2 A.M., most only feeding their addictions with champagne, chocolate, ice cream, and Oreos.

Her overflowing cart of goods barely fit into her trunk. Amanda sat in the front seat for several minutes, ready to collapse in exhaustion. Why had this trip been so important to her? When she got up to shop, she had felt driven; she had to get this done now.

Slipping back into bed - the groceries left in the car to be preserved by the cold, night air - she crossed another item off her mental list. "Things I have to do to make life normal again," she called it. But how much of the list would she have to cross off before it helped, before she could get through just one day without remembering?

CHAPTER 10

"I slept and dreamed that life was beauty.
I woke and found that life was duty."
— Ellen Sturgis Hooper

Amanda finished applying blush to her cheekbones, then stepped back to check herself in the mirror. The pale blue sweater dress hung loosely from her narrow shoulders, its color made her look even paler.

"Damn. This looked fine in the store." But had it? She remembered grabbing things off the rack, trying them on, but not really seeing herself in the mirror. The dress was a size 8 and should have fit. Looking closely at herself, she realized how much weight she had lost, began to remember how little interest she had in food. "Everything tastes like soot," she told Elaine. But mostly, she couldn't remember feeling hungry, at least, not for food.

But that was only a challenge to her friend. Elaine invited them both for dinner, sure that a gourmet feast would get Amanda excited about eating again. She promised all of Amanda's favorites, even to the chocolate mousse torte Amanda rarely allowed herself to consider.

"Aren't you ready yet?" Jeff asked, nudging her aside to tie his tie.

Amanda shook her head. Why ask? Don't I look ready, she thought? She waited for his usual compliment, then gave up. His attention was focused on his own appearance.

Putting on her favorite pearl earrings, she paused to consider that they were the only good jewelry she had left, except costume pieces. Her engagement ring; how could she forget that? Jeff gave her the 4-carat rock, despite her fears that the large stone would dwarf her hand. She had been thrilled then, but now, the ring was too loose and felt heavy. She would have to leave it off until it could be resized.

They set off for San Francisco in Jeff's new leased Mercedes, dark blue again, she noted. In the short time since the fire, Jeff had methodically been duplicating all his possessions when he could. Beyond shopping to stock the apartment and a few clothes, Amanda had waited, uncomfortable with what she viewed as his pretense.

"Jeff," she began. "Didn't you ever think about getting a different car? Or even a different model?"

Jeff fiddled with the CD player, inserting a collection of Bach as if to silence her. "No. Why should I? I liked the car I had."

"If I'd been with you, I could have found something."

"I buy the car I want; you have yours."

End of discussion. Amanda wondered if they would ever get back to the easy way they had with each other, just enjoying the sounds of each others' voices. She gritted her teeth as they neared Elaine's place. Jeff hated trying to find parking in San Francisco and usually blamed her for not being able to conjure up a spot. Just a block past the apartment, a car pulled out. At least one thing is going right this evening, Amanda thought.

Elaine welcomed them in a flowing pair of amethyst hostess pajamas, looking sexy and put-together. Amanda felt prissy in the high-necked, clingy dress she had bought to flatter her curves, curves which had turned into bony protuberances when she wasn't looking.

Champagne sat in a silver ice bucket and canapés beckoned from a crystal dish. Amanda couldn't help herself; the pieces looked like heirlooms and reminded her of the many she had lost. Stop it, she told herself, sternly. What did you want her to do - put things on paper plates so you wouldn't remember?

Amanda went to help Elaine in the kitchen, though she suspected little help was needed. "How are things going?" she asked.

"I should really be asking you that question," Elaine said. "Is it better now that you have an apartment?"

"Yes...no...I guess. It doesn't feel like home. The rental furniture, the things people gave us, like sheets and towels. I still feel like I'm in a hotel. It isn't mine, yet."

Elaine held out a spoon to Amanda, offering her a taste of the sauce she was making. "It doesn't have to be, silly. You're going to rebuild and have your own place, soon. Aren't you?"

"Jeff wants to. And I guess we have to. Some kind of insurance thing, where you don't get much if you don't rebuild. It sounds like we won't get much in any event - our agent is trying to tell us we were hopelessly underinsured. But we fight about it. He wants exactly the same. I want to fix all the things I hated."

"With his schedule, you'll probably get stuck with everything, and then, you can decide."

Amanda smiled. "Good point. Guess what? Leslie is staying with us."

Elaine groaned. "You really needed that, didn't you?"

"She thinks it helps her father to be here. Especially if she can get rid of me." Amanda shook her head. "There have been some good things, too."

"Yes?"

"Like the Christmas card lists; they burned up. We have no address books, no lists of who didn't send to us last year - Jeff's whole anal trip. So we'll just have to send cards to the people we like."

"Or skip the whole thing," Elaine suggested.

"I had a better idea, but Jeff hated it. I wanted to send a picture of the foundation with a note saying 'Santa can't miss the chimney now, can he?' But Jeff said it was tacky."

"I love it," Elaine said, giving Amanda a hug. "You're really all right, aren't you?"

"Sometimes I am, but sometimes not. It just depends. I try not to think..."

"You're lucky you have Jeff," Elaine said. "I don't know how I'd stand it, being alone."

"I guess."

Elaine shook her head. "At the end of the day, no matter where you are living, you have someone to hold you. Someone to make love to you." Her envy was palpable.

Amanda nodded, not trusting herself to respond. What did "having" Jeff mean? She didn't know the man he had become since the fire. Had he always been this volatile, this angry? Even sex had changed. She thought of it now as sex, rather than making love. He took what he needed from her, quickly, as someone eating tasteless porridge would hurry to fill his stomach. She looked to their time in bed for comfort, had thought that this part of their life at least was something the fire couldn't take away. But it had seared away the shield she kept in front of her eyes, to keep her from seeing what she didn't like. She could no more recreate the shield than she could reinvent the photos of her childhood.

Elaine filled the heavy air at dinner with sparkling chatter, cocktail party talk flowing easily from her. Amanda felt as tongue-tied and awkward as she did at one of Jeff's business parties, where the expectation of making a good impression inexplicably evoked the opposite from her. Her self confidence slipping, Amanda took smaller and smaller bites, having difficulty swallowing even the mandarin oranges in the carefully arranged salad.

Jeff responded to Elaine's wit with tales of their plight, but somehow, the stories always turned on how put-upon he was, how he had been affronted. Elaine hung on every word, nodding her sympathy.

By dessert, Amanda felt like an unwanted baby sister on a date. She tried to ignore the growing flirtatiousness, but finally had to excuse herself. In the bathroom, her control collapsed. She cried, choking off the sound of the sobs in a towel.

After a lengthy attempt to repair her makeup and shrink her swollen eyelids, she returned to the dining room. Laughter from the kitchen led her to the door, where she could see Jeff at the sink, hands plunged into mountains of soapy water.

While puzzling over this uncharacteristic show of domesticity, Amanda started to speak, then stopped. Jeff caught up a fingerful of foam and traced a pattern on Elaine's cheek. They laughed, heads and shoulders too close together. Amanda cleared her throat.

She couldn't miss the brief flash of irritated guilt crossing Jeff's face, but Elaine was unperturbed.

"I think we should be going," Amanda said.

"What's your hurry?" Jeff growled.

Elaine broke into the ensuing silence. "An early evening would be nice," she said. "I have a dishwasher - you really don't have to help me clean up."

Always the perfect hostess, Amanda noted, cynically. Placate the wife. Win over the husband. Hadn't Elaine been her friend?

During the long drive back to Orinda, Amanda had plenty of time to assess the evening; Jeff refused to speak and she had no heart to try to jolly him into conversation.

Unbidden, images flashed into Amanda's mind - images of Jeff seducing a willing Elaine. It disturbed her how coolly she could review the threat, as if it were outside herself, about people she barely knew. What does it mean? Was the lack of feeling just part of the numbness induced by the fire? Or was it bigger than that? Was she beginning to question her marriage?

Fear clamped down on her mind, squeezing out the question between knife-like pincers. Amanda welcomed the blinding headache as an excuse to shut down her thoughts, concentrating only on slow breathing. She could almost see the bad thoughts - dark wisps of smoke - floating on her expelled breaths. She sighed.

"What's wrong with you tonight?" Jeff barked.

"I don't know," Amanda said, wanting not to know, not to even consider the question.

They drove on in silence, Jeff becoming more grim and tense as the miles passed.

"Damn it." Jeff slewed the car into a U-turn, then stopped.

Amanda suddenly realized where they were. In his anger, Jeff had driven them home…to Hiller Highlands. In the dark, with few working streetlights, it took time to recognize his mistake.

As they headed to Orinda, Amanda let her developing headache drive her mental misery away; physical pain was preferable. At home, the message light flashed on their new answering machine. Jeff went to the bar for a drink; Amanda played back the tape, not taking time to discard her coat. A clinical voice suggested that she might wish to come to the hospital. Her mother's vital signs were not good.

The fear-pain moved to her stomach, making her gag. How much more could go wrong? In her panic, Amanda wasn't sure what scared her the most - the fear of losing her mother, Jeff or her job. It was all loss - loss of everything that had mattered to her.

She wanted to scream, yet was afraid of not being able to stop. Driving too fast to Herrick Hospital, Amanda began to wonder if the problems heaped one on another were like an overloaded circuit - the breaker had tripped, shutting down all emotion. Even her skin felt numb; she pinched her arm roughly between two fingers; it was as if she had hurt someone else. Her breaths came faster and her mind filled with the sound of them…in, then out, then in, out, in.

She wanted to black out, wanted the oblivion of it. The streets were empty. She would take no one with her.

Cold fingers gripped the steering wheel. She willed herself to jerk it to the right, wanted to hear/feel the crunch of her car against the wall of an overpass. No one would care, she told herself. As she nerved herself to do it, a tortoise-shell cat with gleaming eyes ran out in the street, barely slipping past her wheels. She hit the brakes hard, collapsing in tears on the steering wheel.

"Saved by a cat," she moaned. "It could have been Butchie. I should leave more food for Mom's cat. I have to find him, now more than ever."

CHAPTER 11

"Out of the dead, cold ashes,
Life again."
 — John Bannister Tabb

Leslie Dunn felt frustrated and angry. With Amanda at the hospital most days, she had little opportunity to get on her nerves, to spark a confrontation. A conflict was brewing - Amanda and Jeff treated each other like antique porcelain figurines - but she was unable to ignite it into flame. The two refused each challenge. Leslie found herself forced out into the open, exposed as the marriage-wrecker she fancied herself to be. That didn't fit well with her view of herself as loving daughter.

When she borrowed a dress from Amanda and returned it stained, no comment was made. Last minute decisions not to dine with the family were ignored. Jeff didn't seem to hear her when she itemized complaints against Amanda; he gave even less attention when she extolled the virtues of her mother in contrast.

In short, Leslie decided she was wasting her time. Knowing how much her father wanted her to stay for Christmas, she delighted in refusing him, blaming it on Amanda.

"Amanda irritates me, Dad," she said. "I can't do anything right. Besides, I have to get back. I've missed enough school already." She hoped he wouldn't question her rush to return just as the term ended.

Her father just grunted in response. "You've never given her a chance. This is a hard time for her…for both of us."

Seeing no way to help her father while continuing to attack his choice in wives, she packed her bags. Waiting for the inevitable gloating, she realized that for the first time, Amanda truly didn't care whether she stayed or left.

"I wish I could see you off, Leslie," Amanda said. "But Mom is worse. I'm sure you understand."

But she hadn't even waited to see if Leslie did understand, breezing off in her silly little car to the hospital. Leslie didn't see the point - if Mrs. Creighton was dying, what earthly good could it do her to have Amanda standing a death watch?

As they waited in the airport lounge for her row number to be called, Jeff seemed to be aware of her for the first time in a week.

"Leslie, you know, I wanted to get you something for Christmas, but there wasn't time," he said. "I'll send something over - late, but it can't be helped - if you tell me what you want."

You know what I want, she thought, but you'll never give it to me. "I'll have to think," she said. She couldn't get mad at him; buying presents wasn't on the top of her list either.

As she boarded the plane, she looked back and almost didn't recognize her father in the moody, tense person he had become. He seemed like a shaken champagne bottle, close to explosion.

*   *   *

Jeff dragged the eight foot tall noble fir into the living room and adjusted it in its new stand. Despite long hours of work, coping with a reorganization and the annual budget, fighting with the insurance company, and trying to find an architect, he had managed to find time to begin their Christmas preparations. He intended the tree to be a surprise for Amanda and to remind her that they still had some obligations, despite the dislocation the fire had caused in their lives.

Amanda. Jeff wondered if she would ever get back to full-time work. Not now, not while her mother's condition was so serious; he couldn't expect her to. But even before, Amanda rarely went into the office. Her briefcase, the new burgundy leather one he had bought, gathered dust in the corner by the door. She never talked about clients; Jeff wondered if she had any or if the long absence had moved her back to the status of the law clerk she had once been. She wouldn't talk to him about it. In fact, he had a hard time remembering when they last had a serious discussion of any kind.

He started to make a list for her. Christmas cards, planning for their annual holiday party, new ornaments for the tree, gift shopping for his colleagues at the office and their families... She had to start holding up her end of things, especially with no salary coming in. Amanda had the time now; Jeff remembered all the years before, when they both worked. She always managed to engineer a Martha Stewart holiday without his help.

Jeff wondered if she ever considered how much it cost to support the two of them, how much replacing their things had cost, with so little bled out from their iceberg insurance company. If she couldn't help with expenses, the least she could do... He left the thought unfinished, unwilling to itemize his list of complaints again, even in his mind.

Though he had always admired her spontaneity, easy elegance and readiness to please, he now realized that the best part had always been her self-reliance. Or at least, what he thought was independence. Perhaps it had been easy to pretend to be the woman he wanted, with enough money to burn. For all he knew, her desire to marry well might have forced her to play a role she now regretted. Sensitive to their 10 year age difference, he imagined he could see titles of books she had read before they had started their relationship - "10 Ways to Eliminate the Tendency to Cling" and "Independent Women, Rich Men."

She had also always supported his decisions, cared for him when he was ill or stressed and created a comfortable home for him. Jeff felt bereft; the house always seemed colder than the thermostat indicated and the few meals they shared came ready-made from the microwave. Of course, she didn't have that much to cook with. The bread machine, pasta-maker, wok...all of that burned up, but he remembered their first dinner at her apartment. With only a pan and a knife, she had created chicken Kiev and saffron rice, a mousse tort for dessert. Jeff hadn't really been aware of how much the fire changed her. He felt sure that he himself was unchanged.

He wanted the old Amanda, the one who loved him and who often made sexual overtures to him, so he wouldn't always have to play the aggressor. Not the frump who threw on anything that came to hand, who felt warmed-over food and lukewarm sex perfectly acceptable.

Denise P. Kalm

"She even drove Leslie away," he thought. "And she only wanted to help. We could have used more help around here; she could have set up the office party for me."

Seven 'o' clock. Amanda hadn't called and the refrigerator was bare of anything Jeff felt could be called dinner. He shrugged into his London Fog raincoat again, and taking a last look at the bare tree, took himself out for a meal.

*   *   *

The rhythmic sounds of the respirator and heart monitor soothed Amanda; with each pulse, they spoke of life continuing. If she just can keep going, she'll pull out of this, Amanda told herself, clinging gently to her mother's hand.

Ruth Creighton, never a large woman to begin with, had become frail. When helping the nurses change her position, Amanda had noticed how light her body was - hummingbird bones, she thought. Her mother's eyes spoke to her, though the respirator kept her thoughts inside. Most days, Amanda imagined she saw hope in the steady gaze, but today, the blue eyes plead with her; she tried not to understand what she was being asked.

Mrs. Creighton's lungs had sustained more damage than anyone had thought and her burns were serious. The doctors had hoped to stabilize her enough to begin skin transplants, but infections took a tenacious hold on her system, draining the spirit from her. Even before they attached the respirator, Mrs. Creighton had stopped asking after Butchie. Now, Amanda knew she was giving up on herself, too.

"Give her something for the pain," Amanda demanded of the first nurse she could find. Surely if her mother weren't in pain, she would want to live.

"She isn't due for another shot," the nurse responded, checking her watch. "Perhaps in an hour."

"Can't you see she's in pain? What you're giving her isn't enough."

"You'll have to speak to the doctor about that," the nurse said. "He has already ordered the medications for her."

"What are you afraid of - that she'll become an addict?" Amanda cried. "She'll die if she doesn't get a break. How can anyone heal when they're suffering?"

The nurse fled, returning momentarily with a pale, skinny intern. He looked tired, Amanda thought. More likely to give in to my requests.

"Do something," she begged.

The intern took his time checking the chart, but finally, scribbled something and left.

Amanda gritted her teeth as the nurse hurried out with the doctor, but before she had a chance to escalate, the nurse returned bearing a syringe.

As the nurse administered the injection, Mrs. Creighton mustered a brief smile.

She can't feel it already, Amanda thought. As the medicine took effect, Mrs. Creighton squeezed her daughter's hand and smiled again. Oh, God, no! Amanda realized that her mother thought she was helping her to die. Wanted to die. Couldn't stand the pain any longer.

Tears Amanda had held back for days, trying to keep an optimistic front up for her mother, spilled, painful sobs ripped from deep inside her. The nurse turned the light down a bit and left her alone. Mrs. Creighton's hand went limp and her brow uncreased.

"Do you want me to give up on you, too?" she asked. "I can't do it - I've lost too much."

Too many things left unsaid, too many memories still to be made with her mother. She's never held a child of mine in her arms and now, might never. Amanda studied her mother's face, each line reminding her of the person she loved. Needed, too. I was so independent, she cried. I wouldn't let you into my life.

"Oh, Mom," she moaned softly. "I love you so much. If you can hear me, please give me a chance to show you."

Remembering how afraid she had been of caring for her mother - mothers care for their children, not the other way around - Amanda cried harder, angry at herself for the selfishness, the outright childishness of her demand. "Help me get through this," she had said, never thinking of how they could help each other, share the tremendous pain of losing everything.

But could they share? In the dim light, Amanda noticed the stark angles of the room, adorned only by some yellow daisies she thought would brighten a corner. My mother lost everything, even more than I did, but she only asked about her cat. She never understood what I felt about losing my things, because to her, they were just that…things.

The sudden absence of rhythmic noise brought her out of her contemplation. A heavyset nurse appeared, but only to check her mother's pulse and then, turn off the machine. Amanda noticed the initials on the chart - DNR - do not resuscitate; for the first time, Amanda realized that her mother had never expected to survive this, not once she moved to the critical care unit.

Amanda leaned against her mother's side, imagining the stiffening, the cooling that was hours off yet, her tears soaking the sheet.

"Mom, mom. You can't be dead. You can't." She turned to the nurse. "Can't you do something?"

"She didn't want that, Mrs. Dunn."

"But...I mean...I need her," Amanda said, barely able to speak.

"We didn't tell you, but she knew how much she would have to go through if she lived. Surgery, painful skin grafts - I'm sorry, but she truly felt she couldn't do it. We try to respect a patient's wishes, particularly when a situation is as serious as hers was." The nurse reached out a hand to touch Amanda's shoulder.

"I didn't know how much this would hurt. I didn't know she would die," Amanda said.

The nurse pulled Amanda into a hug. "She loved you very much, you know. Late at night, when she couldn't sleep, she would talk about you. How proud she was of her lawyer daughter, how happy you had made her."

Through her tears, Amanda smiled. "She always thought of everyone else, never herself. I wasn't much good at that."

"Do you want some time alone with her?" the nurse asked.

Amanda shook her head. "No, not now. She's not there anymore, is she? I'll come back tomorrow to make the arrangements." She took some deep breaths, barely noticing that tears still spilled down her cheeks.

"Get some sleep. I don't think you even know how much you have been through; you need to take care of yourself," the nurse suggested.

Denise P. Kalm

No, I want someone to take care of me, Amanda
thought, as she left. She drove home, too fast, squealing
around the corners, thinking only of Jeff and how he could
hold her. It was late, but he had told her he would be home
this evening, with a surprise for her. She had forgotten
about it.

The apartment was dark and she didn't notice the fir in
the living room. Only that no one was there. But she
needed Jeff; why did he go out? Looking for a note,
Amanda found Jeff's to-do list for her. She couldn't make
the minutiae of Christmas matter to her and resented Jeff's
inability to understand her priorities. She caught sight of
her new briefcase, standing in the corner near the door, just
where she would have put it in the old house. Jeff had
dusted it off; it was ready to go. She could feel the
scolding the list and briefcase represented. A perfect
example of how Jeff avoided confrontation, while
managing to make his point.

Amanda remembered what the nurse said; she would
have to begin taking care of herself. She ran her fingers
through her hair over and over again, a nervous habit cured
after college. I'll probably start grinding my teeth again,
she thought.

"I have to do something... I don't know... I can't stay
here, waiting."

Action felt good. If she moved, she didn't have to
think. Grabbing a sack of cat food from the counter,
Amanda hurried to her car. Maybe the best place to be
right now is my mother's house, where I remember her.
The streets were empty. In ten minutes, she pulled up at
the curb in Montclair.

Both bowls were empty. She poured out fresh food and
water, then sat on a stone ledge, waiting. Waiting? For

what, she asked herself. But as she sat, she began to imagine another day, sunny, bright, an April afternoon. She was going up to the door to bring her mother a real English tea, clotted cream, scones and strawberries. She could see her mother opening the door, her smile wide at the pleasant surprise, smell the flowers in her garden. Amanda stood and reached to the image. At once, the pale likeness retreated, and her hand reached up to wave farewell.

Amanda fell back against the stone wall, wanting to cry but unable to dredge up tears. Could tear ducts run dry? Instead, she breathed hard, gasping dry sobs that she couldn't stop. In the December evening, she shivered in a cold that she knew at once came from inside herself. The car heater couldn't warm her, but she had to try. As she stood up, a soft body rubbed up against her leg and began to purr.

"Butchie?" she called. Reaching down, she picked up the rust-colored cat, squeezing him too hard against her chest, but his purr never slowed. The cat's whiskers were singed and the pads of his feet looked sore, but it was her mother's cat, still coming around for his evening meal.

Until pink embers of sunrise edged over the hills, Amanda sat petting Butchie on her lap. Her first thoughts were of her mother, but as the night waned, she began to examine all the assumptions she had about her life. By dawn, Amanda understood for the first time that the person she had been perished in the fire.

CHAPTER 12

"Our doubts are traitors,
And makes us lose the good we oft might win,
By fearing to attempt."
— William Shakespeare

Without the frantic task of replacing necessities and the bedside vigil, Amanda felt the time dragging at her. In quiet hours alone, she itemized in her mind the things she lost, the ones that didn't appear on the insurance list because they had so little real value. To the faceless company, perhaps, she thought, but these were the items that she really couldn't live without. How do you grow to love your television, your stereo, or even the stark teak furniture whose lines seemed so clean and fresh when she first moved in with Jeff?

You grow past certain tastes and want to change the look of your life, she decided. And for the other valuables, most had become obsolete, replaced by new technologies, better designs. Jeff couldn't understand her fondness for a certain set of nesting glass kitchen bowls, each a different color and each tied to a specific use. The large orange one was the perfect size for solo popcorn forays, the small blue one carried only the best leftovers, the ones she wanted to save for herself.

Hurt that she hadn't leapt into the Christmas spirit with him, Jeff had come back with boxes of glass ornaments and strands of tinsel, all new, unscratched and alien. He had teased her mercilessly over the years over her carefully assembled collection of ornaments, but each one mattered, each one had its special meaning to her. There were cross-stitch on canvas ones - indestructible, she had thought - that friends had made for her. Three glass birds, resplendent with real feathers that she had talked her mother into giving her from the family collection. The tacky, glittery star that graced the top of the tree each year always made her smile, long after the mechanism that lit it up failed.

Amanda loved her Christmas rituals, each ornament, each decoration accumulated memories along with age. Jeff might prefer the whirl of parties, but to her, it was a time to stay home, baking cookies, enjoying the spice of bayberry candles, relishing the chance to decorate the house lavishly. Amanda collected tiny trees and trimmings; each year, she had to find a niche for a new one. She dreaded having to start her collection from scratch.

Amanda mourned her collection of report cards and yellowed themes from classes gone by; just knowing they were there had made her feel connected to the child she had once been, even if she never had the nerve to read the childish prose or verify if she had really been the good student she remembered. There had been love letters too, and pictures of the men before Jeff. They defined love to her and reminded her that she had had a choice. She had been wanted, more than once.

Amanda knew better than to begin to enumerate the things she had lost from her mother's house, the treasures she had always counted on inheriting. But her small inheritance - the feisty, purring bundle of fur and claws cuddled at her side on the couch - was precious to her now. Amanda had never had a pet of her own. The cats had always belonged to her mother. Now she wondered why not, when an animal could give you so much love, and by its demand on you for food and affection, reach in and grab something inside you like nothing else.

"But you're not enough, fur face," she smiled at the cat. "I want a child, too." On her mother's last night, the nurse had told her the things her mother had said about her, talking past the pain. She realized that she wanted someone in her life to mean that much to her and that it could never be Jeff. "You can't ask that of a man," she said to herself. "He can never need you the way a child would."

But how? When she married Jeff, she had agreed that they wouldn't have children. Jeff had one; Leslie wouldn't inspire anyone to want to repeat the experience. She had agreed, then, but now, the argument made no sense to her. Every child is different; what were the odds that another would be remotely like his first-born?

Still, Amanda feared to broach the subject, deciding instead to stop taking the pill. Nature would make the choice; Jeff might be against the concept of a child, but once it existed, couldn't possibly hate the reality. For all her faults, he still found something to love in Leslie. She promised herself to make it fair. No temperature taking, or charting. If it happened, it happened; everything would work out from there.

Inspired with her plan, Amanda began to work on their Christmas letter - Jeff's idea of a way to tell their friends what had happened with humor. It was easier remembering the things that had made them laugh about it, and how they had once thought of chucking it all up and living in their condo on Maui, rather than rebuilding. Writing it was like preparing closing arguments on a court case; summing it up and getting rid of it.

"Dear Friends,

Having torched our card lists, we realized that this year, we would only be able to send holiday greetings to our real friends.

"If you see Santa, please tell him we need EVERYTHING. We have a new chimney and stockings; with luck, he has received our change of address notice.

"Perhaps he sent the fire a few months early.

We really hated our VCR - that flashing 12:00 was quite irritating. We never could program the damn thing. In one swell foop, the fire destroyed all of Jeff's old clothes; the ones I had tried for years to give away. I lost the too-tight pumps I wore when looking good was more important than feeling good…"

*   *   *

"I'd like to call to order the first meeting of our Phoenix group," said the tall, elderly man with the neatly trimmed beard. "I'm Mervin Stevens. I called this meeting, but I'm not anxious to run it. Too old. So, if we can get some nominations, I'll be happy to step down."

The audience greeted him with polite laughter. Jeff noticed that some were beginning to raise their hands. He turned quickly to a neighbor and asked the man to nominate him. The man shrugged, then stood up.

"I would like to nominate Jeffrey Dunn as chair," he said.

Several other names were called; Mervin wrote each down carefully on a piece of paper.

"I suggest that each candidate come forward and tell us what they would like to accomplish as chair. We all know why we're here - to speed the process of rebuilding. But each of you may have a different idea of how best to accomplish this. Mr. Handley?"

John Handley straightened his tie and came forward. Jeff thought he looked like a lawyer; who else would have worn a three-piece suit to a neighborhood meeting? He instantly disliked the man. Handley looked more like an ad for a lawyer, than someone who actually did work.

"The process of rebuilding is complicated by the fact that new rules have been established since the time most of our homes were built. We will be expected to comply with the new earthquake standards. What I propose is to centralize the process, establish an auxiliary branch of the city government here to expedite everything. We will create a checklist and provide all the necessary forms, thus streamlining rebuilding. At this point, most people believe that they need to figure it all out themselves, which is counter-productive."

The short speech was greeted with polite applause, but no fervor. Jeff knew he could do better. As Mervin cleared his throat, Jeff began to stand up.

"Ms. Morris? Lucille Morris?"

Sitting down again, Jeff scanned the room, expecting to see a frail woman edging her way to the front. Instead, Lucille turned out to be the attractive brunette two seats over from him. Her peasant blouse and paisley skirt layered over what looked like another skirt, topping sleek boots reminded Jeff of the '60's, but he supposed she had done the best she could with the offerings of friends.

"Hi! I'm Lucille Morris," she began. "I wonder if any of you have considered the problem of living in a forest."

Jeff groaned. An eco-freak. He had read the clothing right, but simply assumed an attractive woman wouldn't need to adopt this philosophy.

"I realize that most of you are intent on rebuilding, but this devastation will only happen again. It isn't the first time, after all. Forest fires are the most natural thing in the world, turning over the ecosystems and providing new and stronger niches for the flora and fauna of the land. We need to consider not just how to rebuild, but whether to do it at all. Some land should not be built on; I propose leaving considerable property close to the forest range as open space."

Boos greeted her suggestion. Others hissed her off the stage, treating her as if she had tried to console a victim of robbery by assuring the person how much the criminal had needed their money. Jeff grinned.

"Jeffrey Dunn?"

He checked his outfit, carefully designed to look like someone who was digging out, but was not normally employed in manual labor. The Land's End catalog provided just the look, with unpressed gabardine pants and a plaid, flannel shirt.

"Hi, folks," he began, greeting everyone with a smile. "I wonder how many of you realize why we happen to be in this situation. Not that it isn't great to get to know your neighbors, but I hadn't planned on wrecking the neighborhood just to accomplish this.

"We live a pretty good life here - mostly we don't need our neighbors like they do in the Midwest. So, you don't know if the guy next door will be there for you. I'm here to tell you - we can only do this if we pull together."

Jeff could feel the audience warm to him.

"The first thing is to understand that it didn't have to be this way. Had the Fire Department tended the small blaze on Saturday according to their standard procedures, none of this had to happen." His gestures underlined the last few words. He observed the audience sit up in their chairs, beginning to listen more closely. "None of us needed to lose our homes. Before we get mired in paperwork and red tape, I suggest we hire an attorney to see what our position is. I propose suing the City of Oakland for improper fire management and for constructing an infrastructure - our streets - that cost lives in the blaze. My mother-in-law just died of her burns; others died the day of the fire. How many more will die?"

People cheered his words, tempering their reaction with sympathy. Never a public speaker, Jeff enjoyed their enthusiasm and caring, and happily, continued on with his pitch. "I'm not suggesting we stand still, but we need to focus on this while public sentiment is with us. Ms. Morris correctly noted that this situation can recur at any time, but it is not up to the people to clear all land that could possibly burn. We can do better than that; we can bend the environment to our will, creating a place where we can enjoy living in nature, without taking extraordinary risk."

Even by voice vote, Jeff had clearly captured the sentiment of the public. Now he would have colleagues in his rage against the Fire Department for destroying his life. Getting donations to hire a lawyer was easy now, and he knew from his experience in the business world that a class action suit was not only easier to win, the rewards were often proportionally greater.

*   *   *

Amanda had run out of Christmas tasks and decided to go back to work. December could be a slow time, except for final paperwork on divorces, so she thought she could ease into it again, organize her desk and prepare for new clients.

She slipped into her office, enjoying the sense of a known routine after being pulled around so much for weeks by events. No new files in her "in" basket, but she had a bit of work to do on some regular clients, particularly women who wanted to periodically revisit support payments. Engrossed in the challenge of finding new ways to argue for larger stipends, she didn't hear the door open.

Mark Hatcher stood there, waiting for Amanda to notice him. He finally cleared his throat.

"Oh! Hi, Mark. I guess I really got going on this," she said.

"Uh, look, Amanda. I don't think anyone expected you back before the new year."

"So they should be thrilled that I'm putting in hours, right?"

He shook his head. "Amanda, you have no idea what it's been like here. Ben Harris got sacked last week - too few hours and I'm putting in 70-80 a week myself. It isn't good."

"What are you telling me?"

"You didn't call in, you didn't bring anything home with you..."

Amanda bristled. "My mother just died and before that, I spent hours in the hospital, looking after her. Just before that, I barely got into an apartment."

"I know, but they said...well, like couldn't you have called?"

Mark's eyes swept past her; she couldn't get him to meet her gaze. "You know something," she said.

He dropped into her client chair and finally looked right at her. "Amanda, they asked me... Oh, shit. I hate this."

Amanda froze.

"What I'm saying is... Well, they hired some new people and... Well... You're out. They voted to fire you."

"And you're the guy with the rope, right?"

"They said it would be easier for you, coming from someone at the same level, someone who you worked with a lot."

Mark fidgeted on his chair. Amanda knew he wanted something from her - absolution, maybe - but she couldn't find any words. She knew if she spoke, tears would come first, and she had decided that she had cried enough.

After Mark had fumbled his way out, she found that packing her personal belongings only took a few minutes. It would have been nice to say good-bye to a few old friends, but she remembered others who had left; people just wished they had slipped out quietly. It was as if they had become contagious and all who came near would be marked for a similar fate. Fear and failure sweat smelled the same, she decided, and taking the back stairs out, she drove to the Claremont spa to steam out the last remnants of her life, where no one knew who she was.

CHAPTER 13

"We live as we dream - alone."
— Joseph Conrad

As much as she expected to wallow in the depths of despair, constantly revisiting all the disasters, Amanda found that the loss of her job only made her feel free. For the first time in her memory, she had no obligations, nothing to tie her to her career or even to the area. Initially, she had hoped for a reconciliation with Jeff, a return to their pre-fire intimacy, but he enjoyed his leadership of their Phoenix group and had little time for her.

How am I going to get pregnant if he's never home, she wondered. They shared the same bed, but only to sleep. She hadn't found a quiet moment to broach the idea of a baby. Their most recent conversation was a monologue on what he expected from her; he made it clear that until he saw changes, she would see little of him.

"What's wrong with wanting things the way they were? Why can't we rebuild our lives as if the fire never happened?" Jeff asked. "That's what I want - why can't you understand?"

Amanda had no answer for him. Things were not the same, and for her, never could be. Amanda could barely recognize herself in the description of the wife Jeff thought he had married; she resented his demands.

"I haven't changed," he said. "It's you. You used to care about me, care about making a home for me. I even liked that an independent woman could admit she needed me."

"I still need you," she said.

"It's not the same. You admired what I did, valued me, wanted me around. I think you care more for the damn cat."

Amanda thought Jeff was right, at least, for the moment. Butchie had clear demands, but when they were met, he showered her with cat kisses and purring. Lapses in feeding, and even the day she ran out of his favorite canned food, were forgiven in an instant. Jeff toted his grudges as if he were weight-training. Each new offense or omission brought the whole load down on her again.

When Elaine called to set up a lunch date, Amanda was anxious to go, remembering how they had always been able to talk to each other so easily. I was silly to worry that she wanted Jeff, she told herself. Friends don't do that. Maybe she can give me some idea of what to do. They agreed to meet at Scott's at the Embarcadero, close to Elaine's job.

For once, Elaine made the effort to be prompt. Amanda met her just outside the restaurant. Midday timing on BART made punctuality impossible; Amanda felt like her nerves were stretched catgut, as she walked in five minutes late.

Elaine reached to give Amanda a hug, but she froze. Something seemed false in the gesture; Amanda needed to talk to her first, before she could respond as a friend. Had they ever hugged? She couldn't remember.

"What's wrong?" Elaine asked.

"The dinner party…" Amanda began.

Elaine sighed. "I was afraid of that. You looked furious, but I thought it would blow over when you thought about it. I think Jeff just needed a flirt, that's all."

But what did you need? And did you get it, Amanda wondered. She ordered a margarita and took her time stirring the crushed ice with her finger.

"You knew I was uncomfortable," Amanda said.

"No, I didn't. We've been friends so long, I was sure you knew that I was just trying to be friendly and social. I've always thought Jeff disliked me, so it never occurred to me that you'd be jealous."

"You're always saying you're lonely."

"Amanda, if I were looking for a married man, I'd hardly screw it up making a play for him in front of his wife. And I'm not. Looking, that is."

"I know what I saw."

Elaine reached out to touch Amanda's hand, then pulled back. "Maybe you never thought about what it was like for me. I didn't know what to say to the two of you. You were my best friend - all these horrible things were happening to you and I couldn't do anything to help. I was uncomfortable. When Jeff got friendly, it helped me relax."

Amanda noticed the "were." You <u>were</u> my best friend. So, I'm losing you, too.

"Jeff and I…" she began.

Elaine shook her head. "I don't think we should talk about it anymore. I'm not after him. I want the best for both of you. What else is there to say?"

The tension soured Amanda's stomach and she ordered only an appetizer plate of ceviche. She barely tasted it, while trying to fill the time with the sort of chatter she normally reserved for Jeff's office parties. I can't tell her what I'm feeling; I don't know who she is anymore.

Even the glass and metal surroundings bothered her. The restaurant looked like a carefully constructed set. She felt the eyes of an unseen audience on her.

Were we ever friends, she wondered. Friends, perhaps, but a friendship that had never been tested. The golden thread she had seen binding them together was tarnished, or perhaps it had never been real.

"You're glad these things didn't happen to you, aren't you?" she asked, focusing on Elaine's eyes.

"How can you say such a thing? No one would want bad things to happen to them, but I didn't want them for you either." Elaine looked at her lap, out the window - brief glances, but telling.

"Yes, but I'm a reminder, a bad luck charm, so to speak." Amanda considered her words, then wondered why she bothered. When all hell breaks loose, you find out who your friends are, Pamela had said. How right she was; that's who I should be talking to. New friends for the new me, she thought.

"I can't believe you're saying this."

"Why? Because it's too close to home? We never talk anymore, never go out," Amanda said.

"I called you. I wanted to see you again."

"Now I'm wondering why. I needed someone to talk to; apparently, I picked the wrong person."

Elaine pushed her food away. "If that's how you feel…"

"I think I do."

"I wouldn't think you'd be so quick to give up on your friends," Elaine said, her voice bitter.

"When you've lost everything else…" Amanda began. "I don't think you can lose a friend, not if the friendship is real."

Surprising Elaine, Amanda picked up the tab for the two of them and ended their lunch quickly.

* * *

Pamela Macklin scrunched the ball of clay in her hand. Again, she ordered herself. Staring into space, she willed her hand to mold the design she had created so clearly in her mind. Her fingers betrayed her once again, and she lost hold of the small lump.

"Damn!" she said. "I'm getting worse. Is this it for my art?" Going to the mirror, she saw the dark circles under her eyes. "Maybe I just need sleep," she told herself. She looked away from the mirror, hating to see the lie. When the muse was with her, she had lost many nights of sleep, honing her creativity to a fine edge.

"Stress is the enemy, Mrs. Macklin," Dr. Hanson said. "You have to be good to yourself, rest when you need to, eat what feels right. We don't have a cure for M.S., but I have seen good results with patients who treat their illness holistically."

No stress. Her peaceful life as an artist, her good marriage, the comfortable home they had designed for themselves - all of this should have given her the optimal environment. It had been, until she began to lose it all, first Brian, then the house. But it was the art she would cling to the hardest, the crafting of beauty with her hands that had always brought the most satisfaction to her soul.

The knock at the door interrupted her thoughts. A good thing, too. I can get pretty morbid on my own, she said to herself.

Amanda waved a handful of wildflowers at her. "Look what I found on the hillside. The hills are coming back!" she exclaimed.

The silly, hand-wilted bundle pulled Pamela out of her misery. "If only houses could grow as fast…"

"I know. I'm lucky, I guess. Jeff has taken over the planning, though I'll probably have to do something about colors and furniture," Amanda said. "I haven't even met the architect."

"I don't know if I'm going to rebuild," Pamela said. "It just seems like too much trouble…owning a house, doing all the work yourself. Renting is easier."

Amanda looked startled. "I imagined you designing a new place yourself. Something that blended into the woods perfectly, full of light and space."

"How poetic," Pamela said. "Are you sure you're not an artist?"

"No. You can be the artist and I'll be the lawyer… I guess."

"What happened?" Pamela wiped her hands on a towel, then rolled her chair closer to Amanda.

"I lost my job. Guess I forgot to go in one too many times. So now, I'm looking for something to do."

Pamela felt relief wash over her like a cooling wave. Someone in need, someone I can help, she thought. I always do better when I'm thinking about someone else's problems.

"No hobbies?"

"Well, I have a cat now, but he sleeps. A lot. I start things, but can't finish. Maybe if I had hobbies before. I tried reading - all those books you promise yourself you're going to read - but then I find I've fallen asleep. I just can't concentrate."

"I know what you mean. I feel like a cricket, hopping from one project to the next. Maybe there's always been some of that in me. But seriously, have you ever thought of doing a craft or some artwork?"

"Like you?" Amanda said, laughing. "I think you're supposed to have an idea first, be able to see something you want to draw or make. I've never thought of myself as a visual person."

Pamela grabbed a fresh lump of clay. "Just play with this for a while. Surprise yourself. If you dream, you can create something wonderful."

Amanda's hands effortlessly shaped smooth balls, then long strings. Pamela envied the ease and flexibility of her hands, but also enjoyed watching the lines smooth out of Amanda's face as she worked. A furless, gray cat began to emerge from the shaping. Primitive, but recognizable.

"See? No problem," Pamela said. "You're a natural. Want to try some painting?"

Amanda laughed, but followed Pamela to her improvised workbench.

Pamela watched as a roughly formed teapot and plate of scones began to emerge under Amanda's brush. Bright daisies glowed out of a glass bottle on the side. She definitely had something there, Pamela thought. Beginner's technique, but trainable.

"What are you thinking?" Pamela asked.

Amanda set the brush down. "I would like to make some kind of memorial for my mother. The stone was Jeff's choice - tasteful, elegant and completely sterile. It's not how I remember her."

"That's a terrific start. I think it helps. I've done a few pieces from the things I found at my home site. Maybe you can find something at your mother's. A collage of molten treasures could be beautiful."

She showed Amanda the small set of fire sculptures - burned pieces of wood mounted on charred and broken bricks, ornamented with twisted metal-melts. The large piece in the back - the one fashioned around the melted wheel of her spare wheelchair - she kept hidden. Some things are too private, she thought. Amanda doesn't need someone leaning on her and I might, if I showed her something that was so much about myself.

"What a great idea! I can't wait to get over to Montclair to see what I can find. Want to go?"

Pamela was tempted. But then she remembered how it had been when she had dug around her own home, dragging herself across the ground, legs unresponsive to her command. It had taken all her strength to climb back into her chair, even using the crutches which had once made the task so easy. She wanted no one to see her like that.

"Not today." Get off rocking your own rocker, her granny used to say, and you'll rock alone into the night. "You came to talk to me, didn't you? And here I've pushed you into one project after another."

"Do you mind? I really did want to talk to someone. I can't sort all of this out in my mind and no one has the time to listen."

Pamela laughed. "Sure. It's been weeks already. Get over it, right?"

"Everything sets me off. I can start out having a good day, and then I think about something, or someone says the wrong word and…that's it."

"What's the worst thing, right now?"

Amanda paused. "I've decided I want to have a child."

"That's the worst thing? But, that's great! Have you talked with Jeff?"

"I've tried, but he's never at home. It's almost as if he knows what I want and is avoiding the confrontation. But how could he? He doesn't want any more children. We agreed...when we first got married, that is. But now, I've changed my mind. I don't have that many more years," Amanda said.

"You <u>are</u> going to talk to him, aren't you?"

Amanda blushed. "I was thinking of just letting things happen."

Pamela shook her head. "You can't do it that way. You know you can't. Both of you have to decide."

"But when? He's never home and the few moments he is, all he does is criticize." Amanda's eyes began to puddle.

"It's not for me to judge, but if you're having problems, a baby won't fix them," Pamela said, taking Amanda's hand.

"I know, but the ticking's getting louder. If we don't have a child now, I may never have one." She took a deep breath. "I'm sorry... I didn't think."

"It's okay, Amanda. I can't have children, but I didn't really have to decide either. Making the choice is harder, believe me. Maybe my pieces are my children."

"I just don't know what to do," Amanda sobbed.

"Amanda, if I were you, I'd do nothing until I was sure. Keep your brain and heart working on it. And wait." Pamela pulled tissues from a pocket in her skirt. "Marriage is fragile. I learned that one the hard way."

As quickly as they had come, Amanda's tears dried on her cheeks and she smiled. "You're exactly right. I think I know what I'm going to do."

Pamela didn't trust the enigmatic smile, but the emotional scene had tired her. "I'm here for you." Amanda hugged her. As she left, Pamela wondered who she could talk to, whether Amanda would be there for her, when she needed someone.

CHAPTER 14

"Joy is a partnership,
Grief weeps alone."
— Frederick Lawrence Knowles

The onset of the holidays, framed by family traditions, began to make Jeff feel like his old self. He had nearly recreated his holiday address book from memory, and happily logged each card in as it arrived. Amanda had been coaxed into baking the kind of cookies his mother always made and the cinnamon-nutmeg smell warmed him. Sipping on a mug of mulled wine, Jeff adjusted a few ornaments on the tree. Stepping back, he admired his creation, the glistening balls so much brighter than Amanda's old collection. Another plus to chalk up to the fire.

It had begun as a grim exercise, but now, Jeff found pleasure in reminding himself of the things he had been grateful to lose. Tools, purchased in a fervor of home ownership, were now melted into a useless heap. Money buys time and services, he told himself. I don't need to burden myself with tasks I hate. Jeff also found he relished thinking about his garage burning, incinerating embarrassing boxes of memories, childhood collections and other garbage he had never been able to get Amanda to

109

dispense with. Why do women have to come with so much baggage, he asked himself. The fire was spring cleaning the easy way.

And their Christmas party had been the best ever. The small apartment was no place to host his office, so he rented a room at the Claremont. Amanda had managed to hire a decent caterer and oversee the affair, taking care of the endless details. Perhaps there was hope that she too might get back to normal. The one jarring note was the dress she had planned to wear. UnAmanda-like, colors flowed and blended over the sheer fabric and whispered around her ankles. Jeff had selected instead a St. John knit like the ones she used to wear, and Amanda had worn it. For a few hours, she even looked like the woman he married, though still too thin for his taste.

Jeff wondered what she had planned for dinner. She was late coming home, but then, they always ate late on Christmas Eve - a light meal - saving the big dinner for Christmas Day. He rearranged his gifts under the tree, checking a bow and then, reattaching a tag. Amanda's gifts to him had been casually wrapped, then tossed into a pile at the back. He mixed them in with his, dismayed at the crumpled paper and sagging ribbon. She used to have a flair for this, he remembered.

Amanda swept into the living room, cheeks flushed from the chill air, a few dry leaves caught in her hair.

"It's gorgeous out there," she said. She pointed to his drink. "Got any more of that?"

He heated up a mug, while she showed him what she had been doing. A net bag yielded up molten treasures from her mother's property; she had been collecting them for several weeks now. He would have rather had her working, but at least she was getting out.

Amanda gathered up Butchie, hand-feeding him some Purina cat chow. "Hey, snuggle-puss. How was your day?"

Jeff frowned. How about my day? How about noticing the decorations, the polished silver tray with the cards arranged on it.

"What's for dinner?" he asked, deciding to forego a fight, for now.

"Let's rummage around and put something together," Amanda suggested.

Somehow, they always seemed to be eating leftovers, or bits and pieces of things Amanda could pop into the microwave. Never a thoughtfully planned-out, multi-course meal.

"I thought we might have something nice - cioppino or a lobster pasta," he said, hoping she would surprise him.

"But you…" She looked up, startled. "I forgot to shop. I suppose it's too late now."

"I don't mind waiting," Jeff said.

She hadn't removed her coat yet. Brushing his cheek with her lips, she hurried toward the door. "I'll only be a minute - or an hour, depending on the lines."

"You might want to make sure you have everything for Christmas dinner, too," he suggested.

"Oh," she said.

What now? Was I supposed to do that too? Jeff shook his head.

"I just thought… Maybe we could go out to eat," she offered.

"We always eat at home." Jeff headed to the kitchen, determined to see just how bad the situation looked.

"No, I'm going. I didn't realize…" Amanda said. She grabbed her purse and left.

*   *   *

Amanda had rallied beautifully, Jeff thought. The dinner, though largely pre-made, had been excellent. Onion soup, crusty with a thick layer of cheese and a crab pasta, almost exactly what he wanted. He vowed to keep his temper, even as she seemed to become more oblivious of his mood. He didn't like to think of it this way, but he had hoped that the end of the year could mark a new beginning for them.

When she decided to break with their tradition of opening presents in the morning, Jeff went along. It was such a small thing, if it meant that much to her. Besides, he couldn't wait either. Working from the insurance lists, Jeff had carefully shopped to replace some of Amanda's good jewelry, a few pairs of Amalfi shoes and two silk scarves. Expensive, yes, but he had replaced so many of his own things already. He wanted to make her whole too.

He found himself as disappointed with his gifts as she was with hers. Amanda's choices bore no sign of remembering his tastes and desires. She had selected a few Jerry Garcia ties - loud and unlikely to coordinate with any of his suits - picked through a flea market, and come up with a few small wall hangings of unlikely value. The worst was a shapeless wool coat - L. L. Bean, or the like - something Jeff imagined he could only wear bringing in logs from outside.

He had anticipated her delight for so long, Jeff didn't immediately notice her dismay.

"Don't you like your gifts?" he asked. "I tried hard to match what you had."

"I guess that's the problem. I tried to get you new things, to start over. You got me my past."

"So what in hell is wrong with that? Are you telling me you faked it all those years? Never liked what I bought?"

"But you see, I had them. They were part of my life then, and I don't need them now. I am trying to start over."

Jeff paced the living room, muttering."But Amanda, that's just the problem. You're 35 years old. You can't start over. Make the best of the life you've chosen and be done with it. You're too old to be having a mid-life crisis."

"But I have to, Jeff. I have no job, no past, no..." she stopped.

"No future?" he asked. "That's a matter of choice. I'm making it work. Why can't you?"

"I don't know, Jeff. I really don't." For once, Amanda didn't cry, but Jeff could see the strain lines deepen on her forehead. "You need to give me time. Give us both time."

Jeff nodded and they hugged, awkwardly, as two strangers might, before finding out the way their bodies fit together best. Butchie purred approvingly, weaving a comforting path between their legs. I'll give you time, he thought, but not much. I've been patient, but I want a wife, not a basket case.

* * *

Cleaning the kitchen after their holiday supper, Amanda kept hearing Jeff's words. "I'm making it work. Why can't you?" he had said. But Jeff pretended that the fire never happened. It wasn't the same thing as making a life for yourself that you felt good about. Amanda began to consider how many things she had done on others' urging, rather than by her own choice. College professors had encouraged her to consider law, friends had pushed her to marry the most eligible man they had ever seen her date.

And after that, she thought, Jeff made most of the important decisions in our lives.

But I let him. She initially feigned an interest in their investments, but later, gratefully allowed him to play with a percentage of their income. He had bought stocks, real estate, mutual funds; she wasn't sure of their net worth. The crash as the glass she had been holding hit the floor brought her back to the present.

"I don't know what we own. I don't even know where I'd start looking."

What had been a comfortable arrangement - they always seemed to be able to buy the things they wanted - now made her feel frightenly naive. What if he were to die, she wondered. Or... But Amanda decided to shelve the "or" for later. In the past hours, she had looked at their marriage, tried to evaluate her husband while they ate dinner; she resolved to re-commit to their relationship. I have to try too, she reminded herself.

The decision made, she hurried to her bathroom, putting on a new makeup and a slinky teddy that Jeff had given her. She had only worn it once, hating the way the thong crept up her back, but it was his pleasure she wanted to focus on now. She sprayed on a musky cologne, another of Jeff's favorites.

Jeff feigned sleep, covers cocooning him on his side of the bed. Amanda slipped into bed behind him, linking her legs with his, while she caressed his chest.

"Were you sleeping?" she asked. She let her fingers slip lower, knowing he would be unable to continue his charade. How long had it been since she had wanted him, had tried to show him that she wanted him?

Clearly aroused by her interest, Jeff took his time, touching her gently, the way she liked. Amanda knew he liked it rougher, harder, so she slung a leg across him, pushing him down into the bed.

"My turn," she whispered. She became the aggressor, moving for her own pleasure, while observing that this was the most stimulating thing she could do for him. She pulled his hands to her breasts, groaning with pleasure when he pinched, then bit the nipples. He held himself back as long as he could - she could feel him trying - then they orgasmed in unison, shaking with the violence of it. Thinking about the baby she wanted, Amanda held him inside her as long as possible.

Jeff fell asleep quickly, as he always had. Amanda rolled close to him, trying to keep the warmth of their encounter with her, but now, his back spurned her. He didn't tuck her hand under his arm when she hugged him. Giving up, Amanda curled up on her side, wrapping the blankets tightly around her the way she slept when she was single.

CHAPTER 15

"I dance to the tune that is played."
— Spanish proverb

Pamela had been quite clear in her refusal. "The Phoenix groups are for those who are rebuilding. I don't know if I even want to."

Amanda had almost begged Pamela to come, so she wouldn't be alone. Jeff always arrived early to set things up and to greet people. Like a regent in his kingdom, she thought. He always found excuses why they couldn't drive to the school together - late committee meetings, conferences with government officials, etc., but it meant that Amanda had to make her own place in the group. She couldn't remember ever having to do that. Somehow, she had always had a role to fill, a place in the scheme of things. Fearing the challenge, Amanda had avoided the meetings until tonight.

Jeff had insisted. "It's like I don't have a wife anymore," he complained. "I'm the damned chairman. Why can't you show some support?"

She had no answer for him. He could never understand her fear. It isn't like we ever really knew our neighbors, she continued the dialogue with herself. But friendships that don't grow over fences might flourish when the fences are burned down. Even though few of them lived close to the old neighborhood now, they had the ruins to bind them. Having never had to search for friends, Amanda wondered how you began. This might be a good place to start.

Small crowds milled around, sharing coffee and memories. They all know each other already, Amanda thought. She recognized faces, but had no names to put with them. Jeff could help me, she grumbled. He knows lots of these people; if he could just get me started.

She hung around the coffee pot, adding cream and sugar to her coffee, though she hated it that way. A young black man approached.

"Uh, hi," she began. "I'm Amanda."

"And I'm looking for the damn tea," he responded. "I always ask and they always forget to bring it. I hate coffee."

"What kind do you like? Maybe I can bring some next time?" she offered.

"What are you - the hospitality committee?" He strode off, his anger firmly welded to him.

Strike one. Amanda headed to the door, then stopped. Who was that person who just talked, new me or old me? Definitely the old person, the helpful, please-everyone Amanda.

"Bring your own damned tea, if it matters so much to you." That's what she should have said. "I'm not your mother." It didn't matter that it was too late to say it; just owning her anger was enough for now. No more placating, she promised herself.

Pulling this unaccustomed armor around her for strength, she marched up to the nearest group. Why does this have to feel like a 12-step program, she wondered. Hi,

I'm Amanda, and my house burned down. The thought made her laugh.

The four were discussing insurance. Boring, Amanda decided. I can chose who I want to talk with. Three other women in their 30's had pulled a few chairs out of Jeff's careful alignment for a cozy chat. Their laughter was infectious.

She grabbed a chair and approached them. "Is this a private chat?"

A tall woman with messy, graying hair and a torn 49ers T-shirt adjusted her chair to make room for Amanda. "Got any good stories to share?" she asked.

Amanda shook her head. "Depends on what you mean by good."

"How about the horrible things people sent you after the fire," the woman said. "Oh, I'm Ramona, that's Michelle and the quiet one is Phyllis." Tiny Phyllis squealed with laughter, her voice shrill, but friendly. Michelle nodded, then pushed her soft brunette curls back behind her ears.

Amanda introduced herself.

"Here's one," Michelle said. "I got not one, not two, but three copies of my high school yearbook. Three people wanted to make sure that I had reminders of how fat I was in my senior year. Even put a Post-It on the page with my picture."

Amanda laughed so hard she could barely hold her coffee steady.

Ramona pulled a book out of a cotton tote. "Anyone want a Bible? Several relatives felt that with all my steamy romances gone, I would be sure to want to read a good book."

After the exchange, the conversation turned serious.

"Have you checked out Firebirds yet?" Ramona asked.

"Oh, you have to," Michelle said.

"We get discounts on everything. Just flash your Firebirds card. Got to take advantage of it while people still feel sorry for us. We'll soon be yesterday's news."

"It's a shopaholic's field day," Ramona agreed. "Phyllis, tell Amanda about that group you're working with."

Phyllis blushed. "It's nothing. Just something my church is helping to set up."

"Tell me. I really want to know," Amanda said.

"We call it FIRE - Firestorm Interfaith Recovery Effort," Phyllis said, her voice brightening with enthusiasm.

"What kinds of things do you do?"

"Mostly, I work with children. It's too easy to forget how much their small possessions mattered to them. To think that they'll snap back as soon as you buy them some new toys."

"That sounds interesting," Amanda said. "I'd like to help, if I can."

"Do you have time?"

"More time than I like. I just got fired. Another casualty of the fire," Amanda said, hoping she was bringing a light enough tone to her answer.

Ramona reached out to take her hand as the gavel cracked.

"Can we come to order now?" Jeff spoke, his voice booming into the microphone.

Amanda realized she hadn't seen him until that moment.

She giggled, imagining him hiding out in a makeshift green room until it was time to make an appearance. She watched his anger build, carrying the crowd with him, fueling their outrage with his persuasive words.

Her new friends took feverish notes, writing down building code numbers and names of officials to contact. Jeff asked for contributions to a legal fund and people began to write checks. He's good at this, she realized. She had never seen Jeff at work; he was charismatic, charming people and leading them in the direction he had chosen. But is it any different than our relationship? He used a different style with her, but she remembered how few arguments she could really say she had won. He made his case better than she could; she wondered why he had never considered the law himself.

After the meeting, most left quickly, as if to get started all the sooner on their rebuilding efforts. Ramona touched Amanda's shoulder.

"Have you thought about what you're going to do next?" she asked.

"I guess you can tell. Jeff's got it under control."

"No, I meant you. Your job. Have you started looking? The FIRE thing is a nice hobby, but you need to work."

Amanda shook her head. "I should, I know. Every time I see an ad for associates, or get a tip, I just clutch. I guess I don't want to go back to what I was doing."

"Then don't." Ramona's voice was pleasantly firm. "Try something new. I have an idea, if you're interested."

"Tell me."

"Just a thought, really. When I got divorced, it was a nightmare. I mean, we weren't really fighting - not until the property settlement. Then, it was like a twisted game show, with my ex and I pitted against each other for the largest share of the spoils. Whoever shouted loudest or whined the most would win."

"I know. I've been there. We tried to keep it amicable, but when it came to kids and property, things always got nasty, one lawyer against the other."

"Exactly. But I heard about something better. Mediation, arbitration, something like that. Both clients go to one person who helps to work out the details. The lawyer doesn't take sides. Sort of like marriage counseling. Some people even get back together, after going through the process."

Amanda brightened. "You know, that sounds good. I'd really like something like that."

"I know I'm butting in, but I even saw a good place for it. I have my office in this storefront in Montclair - I'm a CPA - and they have an office right next to mine. You don't need much space, I wouldn't think," Ramona said, rummaging through her purse. "Here's my card. Call me. I'll get the owner's name."

Amanda took a quick breath. "It sounds good. I don't think I'm ready yet."

"Trust me. You never will be. So just do it," Ramona smiled. "Okay, I'm a pushy old broad that can't mind my own business. But sometimes, you just have to do things and stop thinking about them so much."

Amanda took the card, then on impulse, reached to shake Ramona's hand.

"Going to do it?" Ramona asked.

Amanda met the taller woman's gaze. "Yes. I will." Her shoulders released the tension that fear had forced on them. "Monday. I'll call you on Monday."

*   *   *

Jeff decided to take the long way to Orinda, via fog-shrouded Fish Ranch Road. He found he couldn't keep his anger flaming, while negotiating the tight curves. He wrenched the steering wheel hard, making the tires fight to cling to the pavement. Instead of being buoyed up by the crowd's enthusiasm, Jeff became distracted watching Amanda. She circulated among his friends so easily, warmly received by new people. If he had no new ideas to offer, they would have ignored him. No gratitude, just the usual sucking-down relationship all these volunteer groups engendered. A few do it all for the many. Why was it always his burden?

The engine roared as he stomped on the accelerator, daring the car to negotiate the road at higher and higher speeds. The tires squealed. Gears ground as he shifted.

Almost before he saw the road drop away, Jeff's foot slammed down on the brake. If anger had been distracting, the jealousy was worse. He began to question if any of the Phoenix group even liked him. Just using me, he growled.

This is totally useless, he said to himself. Wallowing around in your subconscious just makes you lose focus. Fuck the Phoenix group, anyway. They needed him. Why would he even want them as friends?

Jeff had selected his friends carefully from co-workers and peers at his golf club. He had never understood Amanda's need to constantly keep in touch with her friends, spending hours picking apart the details of her life on the phone. And now, she obviously felt she had to find new ones, rejecting her old favorites like Elaine on flimsy grounds. Amanda refused to talk about it, only saying she felt more comfortable with people who shared what they had gone through.

Just like an AA program, the Phoenix groups gave the attendees plenty of opportunity to compare their pain and to congratulate each other on their fortitude, all the while failing to get on with life. Jeff wondered if any would have begun the rebuilding process if the tax laws and insurance rules hadn't forced their hands. And if he hadn't been there to smooth the way, pushing them uphill to recovery.

Jeff backed the car carefully off the soft shoulder, enjoying the surging power of the engine. The tires gripped the pavement; he pulled out fast. He relished how quickly the car responded to his command, just as his employees reacted, just as Amanda had.

No! He slammed his fist against the steering wheel. I'm not going to think about it. He tuned the radio to KGO; better to listen to the rants of talk radio hosts and the nuts who called in than to listen to himself.

Having taken so much time to get home, he found Amanda already drowsing, almost asleep. Shaking her roughly, he climbed on top of her, forcing himself inside her. She struggled, fighting the attack, but he ignored her. As she woke, she tried to respond to him, but he didn't want that. He needed to dominate her, to control each movement and the depth of each thrust - to pour back into her all the anger and hurt feelings he couldn't accept in himself. The act felt bloodless to him - he smelled and tasted nothing, nor cared that it was her. He just felt the need to discharge his anger in someone.

His orgasm brought little relief; he couldn't rid himself of the bile he had been accumulating so easily. He watched Amanda sleep, tears in her eyes. She hadn't reproached him for attacking her - it had been more rape than lovemaking.

Her gentle snores only angered him more, as he struggled to fall asleep. Jeff managed only a fitful doze after spending hours making notes on their new home. The alarm jarred him awake, too early.

Jeff slipped out of bed quietly, intent on getting to work without waking her. Looking for his styptic pencil, he found Amanda's diaphragm case, next to the tube of cream. He checked it; she hadn't thought to insert it last night.

He put the case and cream on the counter, to remind her to use it. "One time can't matter," he said, blotting at his face.

* * *

Amanda enjoyed the effort of setting up her new office, arranging for an ad to be placed in the local paper, listing with an answering service and arranging her law books on the new shelves. She had bought a new PC on one of the Dunn's joint credit cards and was already connected to the on-line law service, Lexis. The large picture windows framed by oak branches pleased her. She wouldn't buy curtains. The luxury of a window office accented by trees was a treat to savor, an auspicious omen for her new career.

Amanda had limited her purchases; she hadn't mentioned her plan to Jeff yet, afraid that he would urge her to join a going concern instead. He likes things to be safe, she realized. Name companies with long client lists, history, reputation. Once upon a time, she had suggested he consider consulting, believing that he had much to offer with his management skills. His response had been to produce a budget showing how much they needed his regular income. Mine never mattered, then, but now, some of his money might be at risk, setting up my new business.

Amanda wished she had done more investing on her own, so she could have had funds to draw on.

"I'm on a one-way trip starting over," she told herself with a smile. She was surprised at how right it felt, how much she looked forward to getting up in the morning now, even without clients.

Ramona Prentiss hadn't waited for an invitation; she dropped in, bearing styrofoam cups of coffee. Amanda had yards of computer cable draped around her. She was ready to give up matching the wiring to the installation drawing; the visit was welcome.

Clumps of hair jutted out around Ramona's head. Amanda wondered why until she saw Ramona tug and twist at her wiry hair, a nervous habit. She laughed.

"Oh, I know," Ramona said. "I look like hell. Maybe a green eyeshade would give my clients more confidence in me."

Amanda held up one end of a printer cable. "I'm not a picture of competence myself."

Ramona handed one of the cups to Amanda. "Break time. Talk to me for five minutes and I'll set up your computer for you."

"You know how to do it?"

"You would too if you had a genius Ninja Turtle for a grandson. He refuses to allow me to wallow in computer illiteracy. Myself, I would just stick with paper, pencil and my trusty calculator. Courtesy of him, I now do all my work on spreadsheet programs. Even have tax forms on-line. Hardly a ledger book in sight, now."

Amanda sipped the coffee grateful. "I have to thank you. This office was a good idea - I needed the push."

"Just call me the pusher-lady," Ramona said. "Remember, it's always easier to push other people than to make a move yourself. Call it excess energy. Tax season hasn't started yet."

"I've got the office ready. Now, all I need is clients."

Ramona rummaged through her purse, a contraption that would serve her well as an overnight bag. "I don't know how I forgot. You have mail. They left it with mine since your name isn't on the door yet."

Mixed in with slick catalogs and junk mail were bills for office furnishings. Rather than worrying over how to pay them, Amanda took them as evidence that her office was soon to be a going concern.

A large vellum envelope fell out of the pile. Ramona pretended to be fascinated by the dregs of her coffee, though Amanda could see how curious she was.

"Looks like an invitation," she said.

Amanda slit open the envelope, pulling out a single sheet covered with script and colorful African patterns.

"It's for an exhibition at the Oakland Museum. A one-woman show." Amanda read the details carefully. "It's Pamela!" she exclaimed.

Amanda started to explain, then stopped. How could she capture her artist friend in words? She smiled.

"Pamela is Pamela - you'll just have to meet her. Why don't you come with me? You'll love each other." Never a match-maker, Amanda was sure Ramona's sharp gaze would see past the wheelchair to the wonderful woman she was just beginning to know.

"Wouldn't you rather go with Jeff?"

Amanda shook her head. "Pamela is <u>my</u> friend. I'd rather go with you."

They made a date. In a few minutes, Ramona had Amanda's computer running, then took her leave. "I'm just down the hall if you need me."

Amanda picked up the invitation again. "She and I are getting our careers together, right at the same time," she mused. "Now, if I could just get her back with Brian." Much more fun to help a friend with her problems than face her own intractable ones. "Jeff and I have to talk, soon," she said. "If we only had the time."

CHAPTER 16

"Experience is not what happens to you; it is what you do with what happens to you."
— Aldous Huxley

As a reward for her hard work, Amanda decided to attend Pamela's art show. She blazed through sixty hours of mediation training and had just found a local colleague who was willing to associate with her. Ramona helped her to put together a tasteful ad for the local bar association news and she had sent out announcements offering her services.

With Jeff splitting his hours between work and whatever he was doing to start the rebuilding process, they shared few meals together. Amanda was relieved, in a way. Jeff seemed happier when he was busy, and he didn't challenge her so much or question what she was doing. Seeing her put on a suit each morning apparently satisfied his need for her to be doing something.

Amanda felt a twinge of regret as she noticed the F.I.R.E. flyer on her dresser. When Phyllis had suggested volunteering with the firestorm children, she felt something wake in her, an enthusiasm she felt too infrequently. Even as she began her new career, Amanda had been sure she could squeeze in a few hours to help out. Now, she wondered when she would ever be able to find the time.

Amanda checked her outfit, realizing she had been to few art shows; she wanted to do her friend proud. At the last minute, she had discarded the fawn-colored suit for a changeable silk dress. The Caribbean blue color and the bleached coral jewelry she chose to wear with it always made her think of barefoot, moonlit runs on the beach in Antigua where she had worn it first. She remembered the way colors appeared to melt into each other at her feet, as she and Jeff made love on the lanai. The sensuous feel of the fabric made her feel sexy. A summer dress, too cool for fall, but even the wool jacket she pulled on couldn't diminish the image she had of herself.

Ramona's car rumbled up to the curb, the old Volkswagen too long held together with duct tape and dirt. Amanda blinked at Ramona's attire - she looked like a bag lady crawling out from under the wrong side of a dumpster, from the rumpled paisley skirt up to the clashing scarf she had tied around her head.

"We're going to be the odd couple," Amanda said, unable to see past the costume.

"Do you think the scarf is too much? Couldn't do a thing with my hair today," Ramona said. "Africans like to do up their hair, don't they?"

Amanda groaned, silently. Was there a message in that? Ramona filled her silences with friendly chatter on the drive to the Oakland Museum. Amanda knew she was missing all kinds of useful tips - Ramona scavenged for deals, special offers for Firebirds - but she couldn't listen and worry about this meeting at the same time. Had she been crazy to try to bring her two friends together?

The gallery blazed with the flame-colors of Pamela's paintings, spotlights gave life to the twisted metal shapes of her sculptures. Having only seen a few pieces, Amanda was stunned by the diversity, how the pieces assaulted the senses. She could smell the burned-tar, crispy leaf smell, hear the molten-metal squeals, almost taste the Santa Ana winds again in the air.

Pamela, caught in a circle of admirers, could only return her smile. Amanda turned to find Ramona enveloped in the arms of a bearded, tuxedoed man.

"I know lots of people here," Ramona said. "Like Bert - almost my oldest friend…"

"But let's not start counting the years, shall we?" Bert covered her mouth with a kiss. He swept her off to get a drink.

"I'll catch you later, Amanda. Don't worry about me," Ramona called back.

As she enjoyed the chance to study Pamela's work alone, she felt as if she too were being studied. Turning, she almost stepped on the toes of a tall, good-looking man, longish brown hair drifting over his eyes like a shield. Instead of the formal wear most of the others had chosen, he wore an open-necked black silk shirt, and lean, European-style pants. A male model, perhaps, she speculated. He was that attractive, but strangely familiar.

His direct gaze unnerved her. Shouldn't he feel embarrassed, now that I've caught him looking? He smiled.

"How do you like Pamela's work?" Amanda said, gesturing at the nearest painting. Look at the art, damn you. Stop looking at me. She fiddled with her wedding ring.

"I like what I'm looking at better," he said.

Amanda blushed. How long had it been since anyone had flirted with her? Husbands don't flirt, she told herself. Jeff and I are past that. But his frank admiration pleased her, even as it caused her to back away.

The man didn't follow her, but he didn't stop staring. She could feel his eyes bore through the thin silk of her dress; she wished she were still shielded by her jacket. Grabbing the first glass she saw from a passing waiter's tray, she took a deep swig, then gagged at the taste.

"Scotch?" she guessed. Hating the flavor, but needing the strength it gave her, she finished the glass, then headed for the bar and the wine she preferred. Before she could place her order, an icy glass of chardonnay appeared at her elbow.

"Thirsty?" he said, his eyes laughing at her confusion. The man in black silk disappeared into the crowds again, leaving her clutching the goblet. She looked for Pamela, Ramona, anyone she knew. Safety with friends.

To her horror, she saw Ramona reeling into the arms of one startled man after another, nearly colliding with a small stressed-metal sculpture of a child. Red lipstick smeared her mouth into a grimace and half a glass of wine had drenched her blouse. She sloshed the remainder as she turned, the spray narrowly missed a painting.

"Ramona!" Amanda hissed her name, hoping to catch only her attention.

The sound in the room died as if sucked into a vacuum, attentive ears tracking on the silence.

"Oh, wonderful," Ramona cried out. "We've certainly gone ethnic tonight, haven't we? I'm ready for bed. Enough enlightenment for one evening."

Amanda shrank back against the bar, scanning the room for Pamela, hoping she hadn't heard. Pamela had frozen into one of her own statues, the only sign of life a twitching vein in her forehead.

Oh, God! Does she know Ramona is supposed to be my friend? She's ruining everything, Amanda thought. Just as it appeared that she had to drag Ramona out of there, old friend Bert appeared, and, cradling her gently, waltzed her from the room as if the scene had been choreographed for Fred and Adele. Amanda sighed with relief, then glanced back at Pamela. The artist had gathered friends around her, once again the gracious hostess of the evening. She winked at Amanda, then shrugged.

Hadn't the drink next to her been almost empty? Amanda picked up the now-full glass of wine and sipped. Odd! She couldn't remember how much she had drunk.

"Next thing you know, I'll need my own Bert to haul me out of here," she murmured to herself.

"Will I do?" The man in black reappeared by her side and clinked her glass with his own. "Cheers!"

More from habit than desire, Amanda took another drink. The Chardonnay tasted particularly good tonight. But had it been two glasses, or only one?

"If you're worried about a ride…" he offered.

"I'm not."

"I saw your friend leave. I'll be happy to run you home."

This man - did she even know his name - was definitely standing too close to her. A spicy aftershave mingled with the sweaty musk of him. Jeff never wore any cologne. Amanda drank in the heady aroma, growing more wine-bold with every sip.

"Jean-Pierre," he said.

Damn. He was reading her mind, answering the question she hadn't voiced. Flattering, but scary.

"The party is breaking up. My car is close by."

Amanda hadn't noticed how many people had already left. Besides Pamela, only a handful of people lingered to finish their drinks. She checked her watch. Midnight had to be too late for buses, if she even knew which one to take, and she knew none of the stragglers.

"Last chance for the ride."

She nodded. He took her arm and led her to a cream Nissan 300ZX, a car she had always admired. Cushioned in the leather seat, Amanda began to feel the wine and the lateness of the hour. With a start, she realized that Jean-Pierre was heading for the Bay Bridge.

"No, I live the other way. Orinda." Had she told him? Or had her silence sent a different message? He shifted gears, then pulled her hand to his thigh. She felt the taut muscle of his right leg, then pulled her hand away, too slowly.

Jean-Pierre stopped the car on a deserted street, turning to pull her into his arms. Again, Amanda found herself waiting, staying a minute too long in his arms before drawing back. God! What was she thinking?

"I'm sorry. You must think I'm crazy. But I'm married." Her words didn't make sense, even to her.

"What is one evening in a lifetime?"

Nothing, she thought, or maybe everything. The mere fact that she felt something for this man, someone she knew nothing of, scared her. The tingling in her groin welled up to a flush on her face and chest. The thin silk dress might have been air, so little did it serve to protect her from his exploring hands. Stop! her mind shouted. But not yet, she groaned, giving in for the moment to his caress.

As his fingers reached inside her panties, her mind won the battle.

"Please take me home. I can't do this," she pleaded.

His smile never wavered as he started up the car, but she heard his barely-voiced curse.

"American women," he muttered. Relief washed over her, even as she acknowledged the wetness between her legs and the regret.

*   *   *

Jean-Pierre's car peeled away from the curb before Amanda had taken two steps. The entryway was dark; she fumbled for the lock, having a difficult time finding the right key, let alone managing to insert it in the slot. Midnight was late, even for Jeff. Where could he be? As she turned lights on making her way through to the bedroom, the apartment felt more alien than usual, their few new possessions looked like a department-store display.

Until Amanda saw the three feet of empty space on his side of their closet, she remained convinced that she and Jeff had just miscommunicated. Even after she had searched in vain for his clothes, she looked for a note, a notation on their calendar to explain his absence. Jeff had taken little - his clothes, his PC, a few books. Amanda ran to the garage and it yawned at her, empty of his Mercedes.

He can't have left - what will people think? How can I tell them? What do I tell them? The questions spun in her head, while she searched for some other explanation, some way to believe his absence was only temporary.

Amanda dug through her dresser drawers, suddenly remembering a shirt of his she had tucked away for herself. The one plaid flannel shirt he had taken to Maui, faded and soft through years of washing. Wearing it, she felt wrapped up in the warmth of his arms.

He hadn't remembered it, she thought, as her fingers touched the fabric. Or maybe he left it on purpose, as a sign. No! She refused to allow herself that much hope. Putting on the shirt one last time, she studied her reflection in the mirror, then hacked the garment to bits with the kitchen shears. The thought of Jeff's anger made her smile, until she considered how he might have viewed her behavior with Jean-Pierre.

He knows, she gasped. Forcing herself to take slow, deep breaths, she reminded herself that there was nothing to know. She had not betrayed him. But I wanted to, she thought. I came so close. Amanda hated the guilty feelings that rose up to choke off her protests, but finally let them wash over her, wallowing in the pain. Jean-Pierre thought I was available. I must have given him some sign, some hint that he could touch me.

Dropping into an armchair, she reached for tears she knew must be brimming behind her eyelids, but shock came first. No note, no discussion - how could anyone leave that way? But Jeff had. Amanda felt an almost uncontrollable urge to call his ex-wife, to see if she too had just been abandoned. He never talks, she thought. He just does. Jeff left jobs and friends without warning her, but she had told herself that these things weren't about her. But our marriage is; how could he just leave?

Frantically, she dug through her address book. Late though the hour was, she called everyone she knew, even called the hospitals and police. In the sympathy of their voices, each person told her what she already had begun to accept. Jeff hadn't had an accident, he hadn't crashed on someone's couch. He was just gone.

Her stomach began to ache and wine refluxed back into her throat, burning. She clutched herself, as she dialed the last number she could think of, the last number she wanted to ever dial again - Elaine's. A groggy woman's voice whispered into the receiver.

"It's Amanda - have you seen Jeff?"

"Damn it! Do you know what time it is?"

Amanda clutched the handset. "Of course I do. Is he with you?"

Elaine began to laugh. "Why would I want him? I told you. Now, let me get some sleep, please."

Amanda washed down a sleeping pill with Alka Selzer, then tried to sleep. Butchie curled up on Jeff's side of the bed, filling so little of the space. She imagined him with every woman they had ever known, tried to make herself not care about him, remember how little they shared anymore, but none of it mattered. She loved him. Hadn't she proved that more than ever tonight? Anger mixed with hurt stretched minutes into hours and hours into eons; she watched the second hand ticking into the first morning of their separation.

CHAPTER 17

"The strongest man in the world is he who stands most alone."
— Henrik Ibsen

Butchie wove a serpentine path between her legs as Amanda struggled to carry her briefcase, mail and take-out dinner into the kitchen. "I have to remember to leave on some lights," she told herself. Facing the dark windows each evening, in a place that still didn't feel like home - might never feel like it - made her dread returning to the empty apartment.

As an attorney, Amanda had found her case-load daunting. Hours sped by quickly; she rarely remembered lunch until it was too late to consider anything other than the aging offerings in the vending machines, or the equally unappealing snack foods from the small store in the lobby. But then, she always wanted to come home, always looked forward to her transition into adoring wife. "Now, I have nothing to welcome me here. Nothing, except you, fur-face," she said, nuzzling the cat's head with her foot. "I guess you need to eat, too."

And she had little to keep her in her new office. A few prospective clients drifted in, but none of them had signed a contract with her. She wanted to do divorce and marriage mediation; everyone just wanted someone to settle landlord or neighbor squabbles. Amanda drank more coffee than she meant to and ground down her nails trying to master the accounting software she needed for her business. She had always imagined herself to be a patient person. But after what seemed like hours pounding on the keyboard, she found herself staring at the molasses-mired hands of the clock.

Time was the enemy. She reminded herself that she needed time to heal from the death of her mother, the loss of her house. The loss of her job, Jeff, everything that had formerly meant her life to her.

After pouring Purina Cat Chow in a bowl, Amanda reheated her dinner, planning to read the mail while she ate. The thin envelope from a law office she knew only by reputation scared her. Better look now, she told herself. Knowing can't be worse than speculating.

A brief Post-it note inviting Amanda to call for an appointment partly covered up a handwritten note from Jeff. Amanda breathed a sigh of relief. She knew, had made herself understand that he had left her, but the silence had left her room for hope. As she read, she could almost hear his voice, the tone condescending, as if he were administering a review.

"Dear Amanda,

I think we need to consider whether to continue our marriage. Yes, I should have left a letter, should have contacted you before this, but I guess that was part of the problem. The "shoulds." And the expectations. I wanted you to be the woman I married; you expected me to easily accept the new person you were trying to be. We've lost so much -

I didn't want to lose you, but you gave me no choice.

I'm not asking for a divorce - yet - but I need some time to think. You need to consider what you want, too. Forward any bills to this address; my attorney will handle them for you. I intend to keep on track with the rebuilding effort - we can't afford not to rebuild - in the hopes that we can work this out.

I'll contact you again when I have had more time to think.

Jeff"

The letter enraged Amanda, so much so that she didn't hear the beeping of the microwave, reminding her that it had completed the job of reheating her dinner. He had fired her! She slammed cupboards as she assembled plate, silverware and a glass, letting the kitchenware absorb her anger. As usual, he was doing exactly what he wanted, unconcerned with her feelings and needs, managing to control the entire situation to his satisfaction. The part about the bills particularly angered her. She had to rely on him until her business took off. I have to find another way - I can't ask him for money.

He left her no say in anything. He would call her when he wanted to talk, he would decide what he needed, he would rebuild the house he desired.

Amanda realized that the letter was pure Jeff, the way he had always been, the man she thought she loved. She enjoyed tearing it into ever smaller shreds, as if by doing so, she could obliterate the message. He hadn't changed, she had.

"What do I want from a marriage?" she asked herself. "I never asked that before. It was enough to be wanted and loved." Amanda realized that the time Jeff insisted on would also be time for her to decide if his idea of love was enough for her anymore. The freedom to consider her own needs scared her.

With the single thought, Amanda wrested control back from Jeff. Only one person she knew would understand how profound an inspiration this was for her. Knowing how much Pamela would love the riot of winter colors, she clipped some flowers from the garden behind the apartment building and bundled them up in newspaper.

*   *   *

Pamela knew the perfect vase for the flowers Amanda brought; if only it was ready. Originally a therapy designed to strengthen and enhance small finger movements, she had found great pleasure in sculpting with clay. The slender, twisting column she had decorated with spade-shaped leaves was probably baking at this very moment. Though she had found a good, second-hand potter's wheel, she enjoyed much more closing her eyes and imagining up a shape that her hands would then try to recreate.

Amanda helped her impale the flowers on a frog, which then became the center-piece in her dining room. Pamela rolled her chair to the table, while Amanda brewed coffee. Pamela admired Amanda's restraint; a woman with an agenda, but she controlled herself, easily engaging in the breezy chatter Pamela had never mastered.

I always put it down, she thought, but it's really necessary. You can't just dive into some subjects.

Anxious to discuss her own discovery, she wondered who would take the lead this time.

For once, Amanda appeared reluctant to share what was clearly troubling her. But Pamela suspected she knew. Amanda's eyelids were red and swollen, despite her attempts to mask the puffiness with makeup.

"You know, I wished we could have talked at my art show," Pamela began. "I kept trying to break away…"

Amanda laughed, but it was brittle, forced. "I'm glad your show was such a success. It looked like you made some sales."

Pamela nodded. "Considering the cost of the materials I used, I am way ahead. But even better, the show got good critical reviews. Your name has to get out there; most of that is luck."

"Absolutely not," Amanda declared. "They just took a while to recognize your talent."

"Speaking of talent," Pamela began, grinning, "Who was that attractive man you left with?"

Without realizing it, Pamela had offered Amanda the perfect lead-in. She began to cry.

"Did I say the wrong thing? Did he hurt you?"

"No, yes, I mean, nothing happened…not with him. It's Jeff."

"I wish I still had the letter. It was awful. He says he doesn't want a divorce yet, but he isn't even willing to talk to me. I don't know where he is."

"Have you seen him?"

"When I got home from your party, he was gone. No note. Nothing. He took his clothes."

"What a shit! You mean he didn't say a thing until now? You didn't know where he was?"

Amanda started to protest.

"Forget it - any man who would do this is a shit in my book. You deserve better."

"You know, it's kind of a relief to come home to an empty house now. Well, not exactly empty. Butchie is always glad to see me. But we had so many confrontations. now, I can plan any dinner I want, or nothing at all, spend the evening with a good book and a hot bath. Maybe I needed the time, too," Amanda said.

And maybe you need to be alone for a while to find out how good it can be, Pamela thought. In their few encounters, Pamela had found Jeff to be abrasive and abrupt, radiating anger. Not much of a shoulder to cry on when your life is falling apart, she told herself.

Amanda interrupted her thoughts. "You had something you wanted to tell me, too."

"How about breaking out a bottle of wine for this? I don't think coffee really fits this situation." Pamela directed Amanda to the wine rack and opener and they settled back to sip the oaky chardonnay.

"It's Brian, my husband. Ex-husband, I guess, though we didn't actually sign any papers yet. I got this in the mail yesterday," Pamela said, handing over a carefully folded bit of lined paper.

The poem spoke to her of their courting days, when she had imagined him to be wooing her like a modern-day Romeo, opening his heart so easily to her. She wondered what made him view her now as the woman he loved, instead of the crippled invalid he had left.

"Pamela, this is beautiful," Amanda said.

"That's all he sent. I guess it's a start. I mean, I think it means he wants to try. But he hasn't called."

"He will," Amanda said. She lifted her wine glass in a toast. "Here's to your artistic and personal success."

And here's to your awakening, Pamela thought. Here's to realizing that you don't need anyone standing in your way.

*   *   *

At first, Amanda wrote off her physical distress to the separation. Or maybe to the slow pace of work - she wrote a few wills, just to pay the bills, but it wasn't what she wanted to do. But after a week or so, she decided that she must be coming down with something. Almost anything she ate made her ill; for more than one reason, she had to keep close to a bathroom. She wondered if she had a bladder infection, or perhaps just the flu. Her body felt flabby, but her skin felt too tight, the way a pair of jeans fresh from the wash bound her in.

The doctor completed her examination, then startled her with a question. "When was your last period?"

"Oh, God!" There could only be one reason for the question. Amanda madly flipped through her Day-Timer, looking for the usual notations, but since November, the pages were blank. She searched her memory, but realized how unlikely she was to retrieve month-old dates when she could barely remember what she ate for breakfast.

"Mrs. Dunn. Do you remember your last period?"

Finally, she let the question sink in, surprised that she hadn't recognized in herself the age-old symptoms of pregnancy - sore breasts, frequent urination and weight gain - those things her untested body knew, but her mind denied.

"I'm pregnant, aren't I?"

"We'll have the results shortly, but it's quite likely. I can give you the names of some good OB/GYNs, if you like. It's never too soon to start pre-natal care."

I'm having a baby, Amanda told herself, flushing with the magic of it. Jeff will be... But no, she didn't even know how to reach Jeff. How could she tell him; what would she tell him?Her elation faded as she thought about his reaction.

"I'm no better off than an unwed mother," she thought. "I wanted this baby, but... What do I do now?"

CHAPTER 18

"The beginnings and endings of all human undertakings are untidy, the building of a house, the writing of a novel, the demolition of a bridge and eminently, the finish of a voyage."
— John Galsworthy

Jeff chose Valentine's Day to try for a reconciliation. He knew he had been cruel to Amanda, not confronting her directly. As hard as he found accepting his culpability, he found it even more difficult to understand why he seemed to be incapable of living without her. Anger had fueled him initially to rebuild and to sue the city of Oakland. Spurred on by his Phoenix group, Jeff enjoyed wallowing in the self-righteous anger of the victim out to wage war on the victimizer. But like a days-old helium-filled balloon with a leak, he felt deflated by the absence of Amanda. As much as he had hated the changes in her, he now imagined he could cope with them if that was the only way to get her back.

Jeff planned the evening carefully, even opting for the kind of small bistro she preferred over the more elegant establishment he would have chosen. Romance over style, he thought. He knew her so well. A single rose had been delivered to her office earlier. Once again, he fondled the velvet box in his pocket; Mikimoto pearls. They would look wonderful on her elegant, slim neck.

Initially, Jeff had hoped that Amanda would beg for another chance, though he had made it hard for her to contact him. But she never called and never even wrote to his attorney. Once, he parked outside her Montclair office, noting happily that she had clients. The memory soured in his mouth - she doesn't need me anymore, he thought. He didn't know what to do if he could no longer rely on her need, her dependence on him. She hadn't even asked him to pay her bills.

Where is she getting the money? Stomach acid leached into his throat as he considered that she might have pled poverty to their friends. I could kill her if she embarrassed me like that, he thought.

"Cool it," he warned himself. "Maybe her mother's estate cleared probate. There had to be some money there. This is not going to work if you go in angry."

Unable to quiet his cramping stomach, he drank a double scotch, neat. I need to relax, he told himself, pouring another few ounces into the tumbler.

* * *

Amanda patted her abdomen happily. No bulge yet, but she imagined she could feel changes there already. Her breasts felt swollen, bulging slightly over her bra. She decided she liked the new awareness, the constant reminders her body gave her of her condition. It reminded her of the first few times she had her period; the strange sensations inside made her feel like a woman grown, while her pre-teen exterior kept her secret safe.

She had decided that she wanted this baby, even before Jeff had called and suggested having dinner together. Somehow, that made it all the more perfect. Amanda accepted the idea of being a single mother, gathering up more courage than she ever thought she had, then found she might not have to take on the responsibility alone.

"A child will bring us together. Jeff doesn't remember how he felt when they had Leslie - it was too long ago," she told herself. "Too many fights with her, all interlaced with his hatred for his ex."

Remembering how much he liked her in tailored clothes, she had bought a new suit, but in a rose pink. She tried several outfits in more traditional colors, but it was like looking at a washed-out shadow of herself. Pamela had loaned her some jewelry - a hand-crafted find from an art show. The chunky pieces added a whimsical note to her ensemble and made her smile. She decided that she didn't need the gems she had long favored. Too much to worry about and a lot less fun than the costume jewelry she could better afford.

Amanda badly wanted a glass of white wine to help her relax, but settled on some herb tea instead. Can't risk hurting the baby, she reminded herself. She felt nervous, as if this were a first date rather than dinner with a man she had known longer than any other.

"No. With a first date, there's anticipation, mystery. I know Jeff. We're going to have to make this work if I'm going to have a father for my baby," she said to herself, fidgeting with the polish on her trimmed nails. She scolded herself for the lapse. Amanda had stopped dealing with manicures and polish after the fire, but Jeff liked to see every detail of her appearance cared for.

"Why am I trying so hard?" she asked herself. "He called me. He's the one who is trying to win me back."

The hope of the reconciliation melted some of the steel from her spine. She had been so determined to make it on her own, to begin to make her own choices, but once Jeff called, she found herself falling into the old patterns.

"Stop it, Amanda," she said to herself. "You are doing fine without him. If he comes back, it's just a plus." But her footing on the solo path was still unsure; she didn't trust herself not to fall. Jeff was an insurance policy to her, someone to lean on when it all seemed like too much to do alone. She knew she should line up the arguments, pro and con, like a good lawyer, but this was too personal. She couldn't make herself be rational about it.

"I need him now," she decided. "I can always leave later, when things are more stable."

*   *   *

Jeff had forgotten how beautiful Amanda was, or maybe he hadn't let himself remember. Taking her arm as he led them into the restaurant, he felt a thrill of anticipation nearly as exciting as the night he decided they would make love for the first time. He missed the constancy of his sex life, the knowing that she was always there for him.

Planning to take advantage of his suddenly-single state, Jeff discovered that flirting was a lot easier when you didn't plan on following through. He also had no patience for the courtship; his need for a warm body - any body - came through loud and clear to the few women he had taken out. A large factor in his decision to take Amanda back had been his reluctance to start over with someone new; married life looked attractive to him again.

He contrived to stay off topics that had been triggers for her before he moved out, but that left only the kind of conversation you make with acquaintances. While he tried to come up with small talk, he had a feeling she had something to tell him, but was saving it, the way he had saved the pearls. For dessert?

"Jeff, I wanted to tell you…"

"I have something I wanted you to have…" They laughed, as they both tried to speak at the same time.

"You first," Jeff offered.

"No. Please. I want to save mine for last." Amanda smiled at him. He exhaled in relief. Unsure of how she had taken his absence, Jeff feared that she planned a knock-out punch, a confession of a new love or something else that would derail his attempts.

He reached over and unclasped her necklace, handing it to her. "I have something that will look much better." He ignored the brief flash of annoyance, sure that she couldn't possibly value the junk jewelry she was wearing more than pearls she had coveted for years.

She lifted them from the box. Jeff helped her with the clasp, then smiled, waiting for her reaction.

"Jeff, these are so beautiful," Amanda said. Her tone was studied, wooden. She didn't reach across the table for his hand or try to kiss him as he expected.

"Hey! If you hate them, just say so. I can get you something else. No big deal." But it was, to him. He felt that her rejection of his gift represented more than that, maybe a rejection of him and the life he was offering.

"Jeff, they're beautiful. You know how I always wanted something like that."

"Yeah, but now you don't anymore. How am I supposed to keep up with you?"

Amanda bit her lip. Jeff grunted in anger. After all his efforts, was this evening going to turn into another one of her crying jags?

Amanda took several deep breaths. "There's something I wanted to tell you, something I just found out. At first, I didn't know how to react, but now, I just feel elated. Like this is the start of something for us." She reached over to take his hand.

Jeff smiled back at her. One last try - at least she was trying now. "Tell me," he said.

"We're going to have a baby."

Amanda watched the smile melt away from his lips. She had expected shock, and some reluctance. She had to give him time.

"Damn it, Amanda," Jeff said. "We've talked about this. I've had my family…"

"Yes, but I haven't."

"Did you plan this?"

"No…yes…well, I hoped it might happen, but I wasn't sure." Amanda wanted to tell him it had been both their faults - neither had slowed down that night to let her get her diaphragm - but she couldn't lie. She had wanted this, needed the accident to happen.

Jeff's eyes iced over; she felt him looking through her, past her.

"I am not going to be a father again," he said.

"But you are. This baby is yours, too." Amanda couldn't believe him. She understood that the theoretical concept of having a child might scare him, but this was a real baby. She pulled his hand across the table and tried to rest it on her abdomen. He yanked his hand back.

"Look. I am having our child." Her voice was strident and carried across the room.

Embarrassed, Jeff reached for his wallet. "I don't know you anymore. I'm not even sure I want to know you." He tossed some bills on the table. "This should cover it."

"Take your stupid pearls," she screamed, tearing them from her neck. They scattered in every direction; the motion froze Jeff to the spot.

Amanda took a deep breath, unsure of her next step. Jeff clenched his fists, signaling his anger, but he refused to face her. Stepping carefully to avoid the pearls, he strode out.

Tears streaking her face, Amanda crawled under tables, collecting the pearls. When she had found a handful, she was forced to stand up, facing the other diners. She could see the care they took to avoid her eyes.

You don't hate this as much as I do, she thought. You're just glad it's not you. It shocked her to realize that she didn't care what they thought, didn't care about anything but the fact that she had to stop hoping.

I wanted him to be a different Jeff. Someone kind, caring. I'm not sure he ever had that in him. She wondered if she even wanted the rigid, controlling man he was now.

Amanda breathed slowly, getting herself back in control, until another thought crossed her mind. "Who am I, if I'm not his wife," she wondered.

I can't think of this now, she told herself. Amanda promised herself a Valium when she got home, then remembered that her prescription had burned up in the fire with the rest of that life, and that she couldn't take drugs now because of the baby. Realizing how easy she found it to slip back into the old, sedated, buffered life, she choked

151

out a harsh, hysterical laugh. I don't need it, she decided. I don't need him. I just don't care. She walked out, laughing even harder at the discomfort of the other diners. Show's over, folks, she thought. No applause necessary.

CHAPTER 19

"First say to yourself what you would be; and then do what you have to do."

— Epictetus

In a moonlit room, Amanda sat cross-legged on her bed, trying to find answers in the bare wall across from her. Tear ducts dry, her stomach ached from an ill-considered midnight feast. She thought food might fill the emptiness, but the container of Ben & Jerry's ice cream, the last of the Christmas truffles and a half bowl of fruit only filled her body. The sugar kept her mind racing, when she wanted so much to sleep.

"Jeff isn't coming back." Amanda said the words aloud, trying them out, wondering why she was so sure now. Nothing had happened, nothing had changed, but she knew. She didn't want him back, did she? Not when she remembered the implacable coldness in his eyes as he told her that he had no intention of being a father again. She remembered Leslie; the damaged girl-woman who had to run thousands of miles to get away from a father who had no idea of how to love a child. She had brushed away that knowledge too quickly. Jeff had never wanted to be a father, never wanted to cede his position in the family as

153

the adored one. But the thought of raising a child alone scared her.

Amanda, the lawyer, felt she had to try this case, build arguments to defend the marriage. But all she could see was how much she had changed. She valued herself and her new-found independence; Jeff didn't. Not that he wanted dependence - she remembered how quickly he pulled away when she needed somewhere to lean. What he wanted was a worshipful mirror who could be rewarded with party favors when she behaved.

The marriage couldn't work, but she couldn't imagine being alone now. Fear tasted like ashes, dry and sticking in her throat. Amanda wanted to talk to her mother, to have someone tell her that things would work out all right. But as much as she needed the lie, she knew she could no longer believe in it. If her life was going to work, she would have to make it work without Jeff.

Gently, Amanda stroked her abdomen, hoping to feel movement. Was she selfish in her desire to keep the child? She didn't have to be a mother, but unlike Jeff, she didn't find the choice easy. Faced with a few close-calls, Amanda had always been sure that she could accept the idea of an abortion, but not like this. This was a wanted child - unconsciously, she had planned to have this child. Could she ever be sure that an abortion was the right choice, knowing how much easier it would make her life now?

The readout of her clock radio flashed 3:00 AM, far too late to call anyone. Too late to make decisions, too. But what else could she do until morning? Her mind wouldn't let her rest - even a hot bath and warm milk hadn't quieted her racing pulse. Amanda had rejected books, music and work - each required more concentration than she could muster. For one moment, she imagined how much simpler things would be if she had died in the fire that had consumed her house. All the decisions left to others, no need to try to build a life out of the rubble.

"Maybe that's what happened to Mom," she said to herself, surprised at the insight. "But I'm younger and stronger. I'm not going to give up."

Perhaps she could retrace some steps, travel old ground by taking a job with another firm. The idea wrapped itself comfortingly around her, like the old chenille bathrobe she had refused to get rid of, long after Jeff had bought her a new one.

"I could have the abortion, get a regular job... It would almost be like having my old life back," she said. Her old life, minus Jeff. Nothing she could do would ever make her see him the same way again. The realization that an abortion might bring him running back to her made her shudder.

"I don't hate him," she thought. "We just never knew each other. We never gave ourselves the chance to be friends. But I don't like him either. Faced with the same disaster, I found a way to grow; he couldn't."

Amanda thought of the new friends she had made, most of whom would be happy to listen to her, to help her come to a decision. The idea was seductive; she knew she couldn't afford to give into the temptation.

"I have to choose for myself...for the first time." Amanda realized how few decisions had really been hers. Friends had touted Jeff as a major "catch," warning her that the odds favored spinsterhood as she got older. And I believed them, she thought.

Even her path to law school had been ordained. Her parents wanted her to have her own career and cheered her on toward the "safe" haven of a large law firm.

"I wonder what I'd be doing if I had only listened to myself." But she had never trusted herself to decide, never believed that she could know what she wanted to be.

Amanda noticed pink rays of dawn piercing the early morning fog. She pulled on some sweat pants and a jacket, then went outside to raid the apartment complex's flower-bed. She gathered up a small bouquet to take to the cemetery where her mother was buried.

For the first time, the smooth nap of the lawn, the soft breezes through the trees, the quiet of the dead calmed her. She told her mother about the grandchild she would never see, about her new career, about Jeff. Knowing she could never get a response, she needed none, wanted no validation of her plans.

"It's time I began to live a life of my choosing, to make my own mistakes," she said, softly. "I'm not asking for your blessing; I'm glad I don't know what you want from me now. I have to decide for myself."

As the sun warmed her, she felt she heard an answer, a response she had always known, but never listened to.

"I only wanted you to be happy, dear. Nothing else," Ruth Creighton whispered from Amanda's memory.

CHAPTER 20

"If one advances confidently in the direction of his dreams, and endeavors to live the life which he has imagined, he will meet with a success unexpected in common hours."
— Henry David Thoreau

Amanda closed the last of her case files, then took a sip of coffee. Ice-cold. How long had she been working without a break? It reminded her of her early years in the law office, time passing quickly because her mind was so totally absorbed by her work. Amanda felt exhilarated, not tired. Most days passed with agonizing slowness; she had too much time to think. After weeks of sleepless nights, she enjoyed dropping exhausted into dreamless sleep.

She hurried out to the street, hoping to find someplace that still served lunch. Back when she lived life by her Day-Timer, Amanda packed lunches. Having the foresight to do so now seemed laughable. She tried to conjure up a vision of what her refrigerator contained and failed. She couldn't even remember the last time she had shopped.

Carrying her sack lunch back to her office, Amanda almost collided with Pamela. She leaning on her crutches - it must have been a good day for her - assisted by a blond haired, green-eyed man. He would have been considered handsome by anyone who didn't notice the slight asymmetry of his eyes and how his ears protruded through the long hair.

"Just happened to be in the neighborhood?" Amanda asked, eyeing the stranger with curiosity.

Pamela grinned shyly. "This is Brian… My…ex."

Amanda heard the reluctance in the words, the hope.

"I'm pleased to meet you," she said, clasping his hand, while nodding her approval at Pamela. "Care to check out my new office?"

"Actually…," Pamela began. "Maybe we should have made an appointment. We wanted…" She teetered on her crutches. Brian held her arm, then circled her waist to give her more support.

"You came to see me…professionally?" Amanda felt a thrill of hope run up her spine. Pamela was never this hesitant, this unsure. "Marriage counseling? Or do you need help working out a settlement?" It couldn't be the latter. Brian's body language spelled out his interest - Pamela just looked too happy.

As much as she wanted to see the smile on Pamela's face that memories of Brian always evoked, Amanda also feared what another disappointment, another loss would do to her. Did she have enough skill and experience to help them get back together? For one moment, Amanda wished fervently that they had gone to the best mediator in the business - anyone but her.

The look in Pamela's eyes changed her mind; Pamela believed in her. Amanda led the two of them into her office, confidence growing with every step. She could do this. Ten years of thrashing out settlements in contentious divorces, arbitrating, negotiating and even hand-holding, when a client fell apart in her office - who better to handle this than she? Amanda believed she knew the main reasons why marriages failed, even if her experience had given her little insight into her own.

"Brian," she began. "If this is going to work, both of you have to want it. Both of you have to be willing to work, talk, compromise, negotiate."

Amanda had her answer. Holding Pamela's hand tightly, Brian smiled into her eyes.

* * *

Amanda found the long evenings the hardest time of day. Later, after the baby was born, she would be too busy to care or to give into the temptation of introspection. The thought of a life built around the needs of her child scared her, but she had made her choice. She tried distracting herself with TV and books, wishing to bury herself in someone else's problems. Pregnant, she didn't dare consider the oblivion that the few remaining bottles of wine offered her.

Amanda sometimes wished she shared Jeff's ability to rage at the Oakland Fire Department and the others he blamed for ruining his life. Laying it on someone else externalized the pain. She wondered if he could ever reach below his anger to feel anything else.

Too easy to believe that the fire had destroyed her life when she had planted the seeds of destruction herself. Had she ever really loved Jeff? Or did she love more the life he offered, the image of a relationship instead of the real thing? She had always felt out of step, alone. Jeff filled in the gaps, allowing her to face the world as part of a couple. People accepted couples, but judged negatively those who were single.

What would life have been like if she had chosen Andy instead? She went with Jeff, the sleek TGV, attracted by its speed and appearance. Andy was like a steam train, safe, but comfortable. People envied the Dunns - their life together looked good - but the foundation had never been solid and foundered too easily under stress.

What if she had met someone like Brian? In six weeks, Amanda had come to know her friend better, yet she still had a hard time understanding why Brian left. He cared so deeply, but when Pamela needed him, he ran.

In weekly sessions, the two traced their courtship and marriage, made lists of favorite memories and worst confrontations. Finally, Amanda had them consider what they needed that the marriage hadn't brought them, leading up to the hoped-for realization that no marriage could fill all needs or solve all problems.

Thinking of Pamela, Amanda reminded herself of her promise to use sketching as a means to express her feelings. Journalizing hadn't worked for her; she was too concerned about the permanence of committing her thoughts to paper. But art? Amanda imagined it to be safer; her hand moved freely across the paper when words weren't involved.

Hardly aware of what she was doing, Amanda began to draw, sketching a child perhaps two years old taking his first tentative steps. She could feel the hesitation in his knees, the feeling of instability mingled with desire. Amanda imagined she was drawing her baby-to-be; she wanted to transfer the sketch to a canvas or a tile. Looking at it, she could feel so strongly the will of that child, the yearning.

*   *   *

Session seven. Amanda fought her desire to push the process along. Mediation was discovery; she couldn't tell the couple what to do. For fifteen minutes, Pamela and Brian exchanged small talk, avoiding each other's eyes. Then, Pamela sat up straighter - a decision made and ready to be acted upon.

"I hated you when you walked out," Pamela said. "But I hated my body more for betraying me. You could walk away from it. I never could."

Amanda held her breath. There was always a critical moment when the key issues were thrown out like a gauntlet, where nerves and heart were bared for the battle. So much depended on what the two said to each other, the resolve they found in themselves. She could only be a buffer.

"You scared me," Brian began. "No. That's not right. It was the MS that scared me. I didn't know if I could take care of you - be your nurse - when I just wanted to be your husband."

Pamela's eyes brimmed. "I never wanted a nurse. We could have hired someone. I just didn't want to go through it alone."

"I didn't know how bad it could get. I guess I was afraid to watch you die."

"No, you were afraid to watch me live."

Amanda heard the anger in her voice. She cheered her on for risking it all like that. Brian's eyes were wet, but he hadn't gotten there yet, he wasn't truly committed.

"I still do my art. I cook my own meals, take care of myself. Get the message - I don't need you," Pamela said, her eyes flashing.

"Then, why...?"

"Because I want you in my life. I love you. I still don't want to be alone."

Brian's voice sounded choked as if the tears he refused to shed had solidified in his throat. "But what do I do if I need you?"

"Need me?" Pamela whispered.

"You were always my soul, my muse. I didn't know if I could live without you."

"But you left…"

"I had to know. Selfish of me, but I was scared of how much I needed you. I wanted to believe I could make it on my own." Brian's voice sounded thick, as if he had to push the sound past a clog in his throat.

"And now?"

"I need you. I want you. For as long as you will have me, I want to be with you."

Pamela raised herself using the arms of her chair, then fell across Brian in an awkward hug. Watching them, Amanda imagined she could see the golden threads binding them to each other, threads which had been stretched and tested by her illness, but not really broken.

A wave of envy left Amanda feeling momentarily depressed until she realized that she could learn something for herself from their confrontation. She didn't want to be alone, but was no closer to defining what she needed from a relationship than when she met Jeff. She didn't even understand what she had to offer.

Brian and Pamela no longer seemed to be aware that she was in the room. The barriers were down; they were going to make it. Amanda slipped out quietly, feeling a satisfaction no law case had ever brought her.

CHAPTER 21

"We shall not cease from exploration
And the end of all our exploring
Will be to arrive where we started
And know the place for the first time."
— T. S. Eliot

Jeff hunted long and hard before he found Marv Penrod, a shark in a pin-striped suit if he ever saw one. Marv's London-tailored suit and expensive briefcase inspired confidence; the image of success, reflecting the settlements he had obtained for his clients. Even the conference room smelled like money. Jeff found the chairs too comfortable, denying him the edge he counted on for the attack. His legs sank into the soft cushions, but he denied his back the comfort of the padding.

He could see his building plans go up in smoke when Amanda demanded her half of the insurance money. Marv had warned him she could ask for and get alimony and a share of his pension, too. California divorce law required a 50:50 division of the family assets, no matter what. The roughed-out prenuptial agreement he had made Amanda signed was no longer valid - the marriage had lasted too long.

"Will I never be through with her?" Jeff raged.

Marv gazed at him over his bifocals. "It would be easier if she hadn't gotten pregnant. Child support will constitute a very big bite into your income."

"But I never wanted another child," Jeff exploded. "Can't I do some form of quit-claim? There must be a way out of this."

"If you don't take any responsibility for the child, you'll owe even more in child support. Joint custody is the cheapest route. The courts base support payments on how much time the child spends with you."

"I want nothing to do with it. Can't you do anything about this? What am I paying you for?"

Marv narrowed his eyes. "I presume the child is yours. You are sure?"

"Of course it is." First enraged, Jeff then began to consider the implications. "And if it isn't?"

"You're off the hook. Usually."

But it had to be his. Amanda wouldn't cheat. She didn't like sex that much. He laughed at the idea of Amanda in the arms of someone else, but it was a bitter laugh. He remembered a time when she had been an enthusiastic partner, or had she just been a better actress than he gave her credit for?

Stomach acid welled up, tasting bitter on his tongue. He would make her so miserable, she wouldn't even try to challenge the low-ball offer he planned to make. Jeff was sure she knew little about his investments - money he should be able to hide, with his lawyer's help. She had expressed little interest in acquiring anything she couldn't see or touch.

Amanda entered the conference room alone.

"Where's your lawyer?" Jeff challenged.

"I hoped I wouldn't need one," she said. "At least, not for the first meeting. The truth is, I didn't want to waste the money if we could come to an agreement."

Not waiting for his attorney's guidance, Jeff shoved his offer letter across the table. "This is as good as it gets," he said, his voice echoing the sneer on his face.

Amanda studied the document, reading each line slowly. Although it could only have been a few minutes, Jeff wanted to rush her, to force her into signing without thinking too much about it. He wanted her to be emotional - to forget that she had once done this to other people as their lawyer. He squirmed in his seat, hating to have ceded control of the situation by making the first offer.

"It's come to this, then," she said. "This is all that's left of us." She shook her head.

"Don't get maudlin. It's fair, and most important, it means we won't have to communicate after this." Jeff could hear how defensive his voice sounded, knew he couldn't muster believability into the idea that it was a reasonable offer.

Amanda took a pen from the desk set and signed the paper. She stood up. "It isn't fair and you know it. Don't think you're fooling me. You'd never make things easier for me and your child; you're only doing this minimal settlement because the law requires it. But guess what? I don't care." She slid the paper back to him.

"That's it?" Marv said, shocked. "Don't you want to discuss it first?"

"Whose side are you on?" Jeff screamed. "She signed it, you idiot. You made easy money today."

"But you said nothing about child support," Marv said, scanning the agreement. "Jeff, I prepared something. The two of you should at least discuss it."

Amanda stared at the second document. "Jeff wants nothing to do with our child, and, having gotten to know Leslie, perhaps that's best."

"What do you know about raising children?" Jeff asked.

Marv pushed Jeff back into his chair. "Settle down. It's over now. Don't start a fight now."

Amanda rose to her feet. "I know your work, Marv. Jeff wouldn't have hired you if he wanted a real settlement conference. You're a steamroller. I might win more if I fight this, but at what cost?"

"Amanda, wait," Jeff shouted at her back. "It doesn't have to be like this."

Amanda's sad smile was so heart-breakingly beautiful that Jeff began to regret his haste. Maybe she would have considered an abortion. Did he really want to lose her?

"I think it had to be exactly like this. I needed to see what I meant to you - obligation and responsibility. And how far you were willing to go, how little I meant to you. I guess at some point, I may thank you for that."

Amanda's dignified exit left Jeff speechless. He clutched the document in his hand, but not with the grip of a victor, as he had expected. His triumph felt empty, as if he had reached out to claim his enemy's sword and found he held only a tin replica.

* * *

"It's the strangest thing, Pamela," Amanda said, taking another sip of cappuccino. "I feel free. As if all the things I owned, all the parts of my life that defined me really just weighed me down. I want to be depressed, because it's what I expected to feel, but I'm almost elated."

Pamela smiled. "We're both at a cross-roads, a new beginning. We can choose the path we want, but with a lot more knowledge and experience than when we set out in our 20's."

"I think that's why I didn't fight Jeff. I thought the sight of his lawyer would bring out something in me, but it didn't. If I had a killer instinct, it's gone now. I had the strangest feeling that if I fought this, no matter how it came out, I couldn't win. Once in a while, I had a client who refused to fight for what I knew we could win for her. I never understood it; I think I do now."

"It's funny," Pamela said. "Do you know that Brian and I never really got around to discussing a settlement? Almost as if we knew how final that would be. And then the fire wiped out everything we had, so the point was moot. I'm glad we never went through that; sorting through the remains of a relationship could only be painful."

"I don't miss having my wedding pictures. I always wondered what you were supposed to do with them, after a divorce. Use them for a dart board?" Amanda said.

"And since mine are gone, I have a good excuse to get new ones at our rededication ceremony. Which we wouldn't be having without you."

"I can't think of anything I've done in this career or my last that made me happier. Hey, I'm not supposed to feel happy, am I? I just got divorced."

"Why not? It's a beautiful day, pregnancy makes you look so vibrant, and we're in this pretty street cafe eating cholesterol bomb desserts," Pamela said, her gesture taking it all in. "We make our happiness. It isn't something that just happens when you're not looking."

167

"The oddest thing is that I really want to hate Jeff. But I don't." Amanda paused. "Mostly, I feel sorry for him. He wants something he can't have - things will never go back to the way they were before the fire - and nothing else will work for him. He's so angry. Every line of his offer sounded defensive. 'Mine, mine, mine.' I wonder if he thinks all that money will keep him warm at night."

"If not that, then his anger will."

"How did you feel...when Brian left you? How did you manage to want him again?"

Pamela took a deep swallow of her coffee. "That's a tough one. I was incredibly depressed when he left, but I never hated him, never stopped wanting him. Hell, I wanted to leave myself, too. And in some ways, he was never out of my life. He kept in touch, sent me money and gifts. I thought I was kidding myself, but I always believed he might come back. I kept the welcome mat out to keep myself sane. I pretended he still wanted me. I'll never know what made him come back. If anything, I'm worse off than when he left. Physically, that is."

"I keep forgetting that there's anything wrong with you. I'm sorry. That probably came out wrong. But the MS doesn't seem to have anything to do with who you are," Amanda said.

"Thank you. Oh, I still have some horrendously bad days, remembering what I could do with my art and can't anymore. But mostly, it's a whole lot better than the alternative."

"We're survivors, you and I," Amanda said. The word made her think about the ones that didn't make it, like her mother. She wondered if the person she was now could have talked her mother into fighting harder. She barely recognized herself in the frightened woman who had felt her mother's injuries were just one more burden, one more hurdle to struggle over, when she so badly wanted someone to lean on.

"Heroes, really," Pamela said, squeezing Amanda's hand across the table. "Heroes are just regular folks who scrabble their way through adversity and come out better on the other side."

CHAPTER 22

"To finish the moment, to find the journey's end
in every step of the road, to live the greatest number
of good hours is wisdom."
— Emerson

Jeff sat at the bar at the Claremont Hotel, sipping his third scotch. The panoramic San Francisco Bay view stretching intact and undamaged from Oakland to El Cerrito allowed him to pretend for a few moments that nothing had happened. Behind the hotel, the scarred hillside looked as devastated as the day they had returned from Hawaii. Months had passed, but his Phoenix group had barely begun to slog through the paperwork, insurance and legal issues. The City of Oakland employees appeared to relish the opportunity to block their progress, at least in Jeff's mind, and the state was no better. Now, they were talking about the capital gains tax implications of the insurance pay-offs.

"Kick'em when they're down," he muttered.

"Huh?" The businessman next to him looked at the television, then at Jeff, trying to interpret the comment.

"When I talk to you, you'll know it," Jeff said, his eyes narrowing.

"Hey! Tell it to the bartender." The man picked up his drink and moved to a table.

You can afford to be a jerk, Jeff thought. Bet your house is intact. And your wife is probably cooking you dinner, too. He missed the occasional gourmet spreads Amanda created for him, even though they had dined out more than they ate in. In the intervals before and between marriages, he had never bothered to learn to cook. And I'm not about to start now, he grumbled, careful this time not to make his gripe audible.

Maybe it was time to start looking for likely wife prospects. Jeff liked having his needs seen to. With the money he had squirreled away - no, be honest; the money Amanda had let him keep - he should be able to attract someone who was willing to be very nice to him to improve her lifestyle. Not another blonde, he decided. Too sure of themselves, too polished. He liked them hungrier, more grateful. He glanced around the room, noting how many women were sitting with other women, how few were with dates. Easy pickings, he thought. But not tonight.

He downed the last of his drink, paid the tab and summoned the valet for his car. From the parking lot, he could see the blackened trees, the fractured foundations. As he pulled out a dollar for the tip, a picture of Amanda fell from his wallet. Dressed in a slim, silk envelope of watercolors, she leaned against a palm tree, smiling at the camera. At him. He began to crumple the picture, then, thinking better of it, slipped it behind a credit card for safe-keeping.

*   *   *

Denise P. Kalm

Arriving early at the Piedmont Community Center to help set up, Amanda decided that Pamela and Brian had been wise to wait until the beginning of May to repeat their vows. The weather was perfect. The glass-enclosed center nestled in a cleft in the hill, surrounded by tiered beds of blooming flowers and greenery, more than anyone would consider buying, even for a wedding. The center was small, but perfect for the few friends the couple had chosen to invite.

Amanda tugged at her dress. The sheath pulled across her belly and her breasts. Time to start shopping again, focusing on flowing dresses and drawstrings or elastic waists. An unappealing thought; she hadn't been able to recapture her love of shopping since the fire. The Amanda of old could drop by the malls two or three times a week, putting an outfit together. Now, she sought out timeless styles and fabrics, ensuring she need shop only rarely.

Pamela looked radiant in a gold and amber Dashiki. Brian wore a embroidered silk overshirt. As the ceremony began, he helped Pamela out of her chair; she leaned against him as they retold their vows and recited poetry they had written. Tissues blotting eyes didn't hide the smiles that echoed her own. She enjoyed knowing that she had contributed to this moment.

Sipping punch, Amanda circulated, sure that she would find new friends among the guests. A stocky, bearded man tried to catch her eye. She was sure he had been looking at her before. His large hands completely enveloped the small punch cup, his suit strained across his broad shoulders, as if it had been borrowed from a smaller man. He smiled at her, but didn't approach.

Damn, she thought. I must look awful. The wind had blown her hair and she knew that tears had destroyed her eye makeup. Maybe that's why he's looking, wondering who the raccoon came with. Her dress felt even tighter than usual. She pulled in her stomach and tried to paste a who-cares-what-I-look-like smile on her face.

The bearded man toasted her with his glass and his eyes twinkled. If he's so interested, why isn't he coming over to me, she wondered? She was accustomed to having men seek her out, even after her marriage to Jeff. Amanda didn't make the approach; she didn't have to. Besides, he wasn't her type at all, too messy-looking and heavier than she liked.

But she couldn't stop looking at him. Finally, intrigued by his patience and attracted by the gentle air of friendliness he exuded, Amanda made her way to him, deciding that she had to begin breaking all her old rules. If you see someone interesting, go meet him, she told herself. Even if he isn't that interesting, go anyway.

He clasped her hand in both of his. "Martin Brandt," he said. "And you must be Amanda. Pamela speaks of you often."

Amanda blushed. Had Pamela been playing matchmaker? Why hadn't she mentioned Martin to her?

"Have you known her long?"

"For years. She and Brian helped to finance my business, a software company. I write programs for small and home-based businesses."

"Maybe you could help me figure out my system," she said. "I'm trying to automate my office - it's making me nuts." Oh, God! How could she be so pushy? It was like asking a doctor for a diagnosis at a party.

"Of course I can. But there's a caveat - I always try to sell my own systems," he said, laughing.

Nice move, she thought. Martin had defused the situation effortlessly, making her feel at ease.

"What kind of business is it?" he asked, and they began the feint and parry of new acquaintances, sharing the best of themselves. Amanda began to relax.

"I'm divorced," she said. "I noticed you checking out my ring finger."

"Only after you checked mine," he said.

"You weren't supposed to notice. Besides, you could still be married. Many men don't wear rings."

"I could be. But I'm not. Not anymore," Martin said.

"Mine isn't even final yet," Amanda confessed.

"The first year's the hardest, especially if you have kids."

Amanda smiled. "Do you?"

Brian laughed. "Well, they'd hate it if I called them kids anymore, but yes. Two young adults. They're great. Just past the point of thinking the old folks don't know anything, but young enough to still need to drop by for a handout or a free meal."

Amanda liked his warmth when he spoke of his children. It made her brave. "I'm having a baby," she said.

"Then you've got to be as uncomfortable in your party duds as I am. As I recall, there are some nice-looking maternity pants and smocks out there. You'd look great in something like that."

Amanda giggled at the thought of looking great in any baggy outfit. "Do you think so?"

"Yeah. I'd definitely give you a second look."

Amanda blushed.

"That blush would go great with a checked smock. Just the thing to wear to a picnic. Want to share a picnic blanket with me? I can rustle up a nice wine and cheese picnic."

A shiver ran up her spine. It sounded like he was asking her for a date. As she looked into his eyes, she realized that he meant to make the offer casual, to keep the pressure off.

"When it gets warmer, maybe," she said.

Martin immediately changed the subject, telling her more about his company, then about his family. Amanda envied him his close family ties. She had aunts and uncles, nieces and nephews, but would have to hunt to track any of them down. That might not be a bad idea, she thought, making a mental note.

Hearing his family stories made her remember how alone she felt when she thought about her life after the baby was born. Someone like Martin would take care of me, she thought. He had already expressed a great deal of interest in her child, as if he liked the thought of another baby.

"There's always someone with a little one in my family," he had said. "Don't know what we would do around Christmas or Easter without the children to plan for."

Amanda thought she would be safe with Martin. The caustic edge that had crept into Jeff's voice even in their early dates was absent in Martin's voice. She imagined being shielded by Martin's strength and kindness.

"Hey, I know it's a little premature, but I'd love to have your phone number. I mean, before you run away," Martin asked, suddenly shy.

Amanda wondered if he could read her thoughts. She had half-envisioned a life with him even before their first date and now he was waiting on her to take the first step. Easier to rush ahead in my mind, she thought.

She began to fumble in her purse for a business card, then stopped. Wasn't this the old Amanda, going with the easy out, looking for a protector? As much as she craved the security a relationship would offer her and her child, as much as she wanted a man, she knew she wasn't ready. Maybe he wasn't either.

What would I be giving him, what would I be bringing to the relationship, she wondered. I haven't really started to like myself, but I'm so willing to have someone tell me I'm wonderful, give me the self-esteem I can't yet find in myself.

Amanda smiled up at him. "Martin, I'm just not ready for this yet," she said. "Maybe later. I need to get myself together first."

Martin gave her a gentle hug. "When you are, I'll be here."

Thank you, she whispered to him in her mind. But I won't be ready for you or anyone until I no longer need a safety net.

ABOUT THE AUTHOR

Denise P. Kalm has been writing since 1990, specializing in political commentary. Her work appears regularly in San Francisco Bay Area newspapers and political magazines. Travel writing, scuba diving, and genre fiction are other areas of interest. Ms. Kalm has regular columns in *New Horizons* and *Libertarian Lifeline* and has been published in *"Discover Diving"* and *"Cruise Travel."* Her short horror fiction has been published in the small press and tales of computer people 'on the edge' have appeared in national magazines such as *"Moxie."*

When her mother and many friends lost their homes in the '91 Oakland Firestorm, Ms. Kalm was inspired to write about the tragedy. Through research and interviews, she developed a novel based on the changes people make when they experience major losses in their lives. Though a work of fiction, *"LIFESTORM"* draws heavily from real-life reactions and events in this disaster.

"LIFESTORM is Ms. Kalm's first novel. Based on her studies in biochemical genetics, a biomedical technothriller, *"EXECUTIVE PRIVILEGE,"* is in the works, as is *"TWISTING IN THE WIND,"* a collection of horror stories. Ms. Kalm resides in Walnut Creek, California, with her pet rabbit and PC.